'Written with obvious affection and admiration, this is a moving portrait of a philosophical and visionary man who was also pragmatic enough to know that anger and revenge would destroy South Africa.'

*Booklist*

ALSO BY JOHN CARLIN

*Playing the Enemy: Nelson Mandela and
the Game That Made a Nation*

# Knowing
# Mandela

## JOHN CARLIN

Atlantic Books
London

First published in the United States of America in 2013 by
Harper Perennial, an imprint of HarperCollins Publishers LLC.

First published in Great Britain in 2013 by Atlantic Books,
an imprint of Atlantic Books Ltd.

This paperback edition published in 2014 by Atlantic Books.

10 9 8 7 6 5 4 3 2 1

A CIP catalogue record for this book is available from the British Library.

Hardback ISBN: 978-1-78239-432-7
E-book ISBN: 978-178239-433-4
Paperback ISBN: 978-1-78239-434-1

Designed by William Ruoto
Title page photograph © David Goldblatt
Printed in Great Britain.

Atlantic Books
An Imprint of Atlantic Books Ltd
Ormond House
26–27 Boswell Street
London
WC1N 3JZ

www.atlantic-books.co.uk

*For South Africa*

## Mandela's Cell

I stood among a crowd
of tourists from abroad
and stared into his past:

a cage of bricks and bars
as gloomy and as cramped
as racial bias in the mind,

and in that narrow tomb
a bench, a gleam of bowl,
a stone-cold strip of floor.

I could not hear the clang
shook from a gate of steel
that bigotry kept locked,

nor see a gaunt-faced man
fold up each dawn for years
the mat on which he'd dreamed.

Instead, far off, I heard
the cheering of the world
when he the era's Lazarus

walked out into the sun.

Around that unlocked gate,
that legacy's stark shrine
the cameras flashed applause.

Chris Mann

# CONTENTS

# PREFACE

This is a short book about a big man I was fortunate to get to know, Nelson Mandela. The story centers on the epic period, between 1990 and 1995, when Mandela faced his most daunting obstacles and achieved his greatest triumphs; the time when the full flower of his genius as a political leader was most vividly on display.

I spent those five years recording Mandela's feats, trials, and tribulations as the South African correspondent for the *London Independent* and, as such, was one of the few foreign journalists there to cover both his release from prison, on February 11, 1990, and his accession to the presidency four years later. My proximity to Mandela throughout this decisive period in South Africa's history allowed me to observe the man as closely as anyone in my position could reasonably have expected. I don't presume to call him a friend, but I can safely say that he knew very well who I was, and read much of what I wrote, which fills me with pride.

After I left South Africa for Washington in 1995, I continued to study and think about Mandela in the course of interviewing many people who had been close to him as research for a number of film documentaries and for my previous book, *Playing the Enemy*, about his crowning political moment, a turning point in history masquerading as a game of rugby. I have accumulated an enormous amount of information, along with many telling anecdotes about Mandela that have shaped my perceptions about his private and public life.

I believe that, large as Mandela's presence on the global stage has been, there's still much more to say about the man, the quality of his leadership, and the legacy he leaves the world. My hope is that readers will come away from this book with a more profound understanding of Mandela the individual and of why he has been the towering moral and political figure of our age.

Yet he had his flaws and bore the scars of much personal anguish. His triumphs on the political stage were won at the cost of unhappiness, loneliness, and disappointment. He was neither a superman nor a saint. But this only serves, in my view, to magnify his achievement, placing him alongside men like Abraham Lincoln, Mahatma Gandhi, and Martin Luther King, Jr. on the sparsely populated pantheon of historical greats.

General Alan Brooke, Britain's Chief of the Imperial General Staff during the Second World War, said of Winston Churchill, "He is quite the most wonderful man I have ever met, and it is a source of never-ending interest studying him and getting to realize that occasionally such human beings make their appearance on this earth, human beings who stand out head and shoulders above all others."

To me, those words may as well have been said, with at least as much relevance, about Mandela. He is the one political leader I have encountered in more than thirty years as a journalist—reporting on conflicts all over the world, from bloody guerrilla warfare in Central America to bloodless battles of words in the U.S. Congress—who succeeded in upending the cynicism that tends to go hand in hand with the business of journalism. I arrived in South Africa after ten years in Latin America, sickened by the horrors wrought by murderous generals on their own people and by the puppet presidents put in place by Cold War powers. Mandela changed all that. Thanks to him, I left South Africa newly convinced that noble and enlightened leadership had not, after all, been erased from the roster of human possibilities.

Just about everywhere we look, our faith in political leaders has hit rock bottom; mediocrity, fanaticism, and moral cowardice abound. Nelson Mandela, who remained as generous as he was shrewd, despite spending twenty-seven years in jail, stands as a timely reminder and a timeless inspiration. Humanity is, and always has been, capable of great things, and there is always room and reason for us to do better.

With gratitude and affection, I submit this attempt to capture Mandela's imperishable legacy in words.

August 2013

1

# THE PRESIDENT AND
# THE JOURNALIST

**C**ondemned in 1964 to life in prison for taking up arms against the state, he was supposed to have died in a small cell on a small island. Yet here was Nelson Mandela, almost thirty years later, standing before me, no longer a prisoner of that state, but the head of it. Barely a month had passed since he had been elected president of South Africa when he welcomed me into his new office at the Union Buildings in Pretoria, wearing his large and familiar smile, enveloping my hand in his enormous one, leathery after years of forced labor. "Ah, hello, John!" he cried with what felt like genuine delight. "How are you? Very good to see you."

It was flattering to have the most celebrated man in the world call me by my first name with such seemingly spontaneous exuberance but, for the hour I spent with him, in the first interview he did with a foreign newspaper after assuming power, I chose to forget that Mandela, like that other master politician Bill Clinton, seemed able to recollect the name of

1

virtually every person he'd ever met. It was only later, when the glow of his charm had worn off, that I paused to consider whether his behavior was calculated, whether he had deliberately sought to beguile me, as he had succeeded in doing with every other journalist, every politician of every hue, practically every single person who had spent any time in his company. Was he an actor or was he sincere? I'd come up with an answer in due time, but the honest truth is that, back then, I, like all the others, was powerless to resist.

Six foot tall, commandingly upright in a dark, pencil-sharp suit, Mandela walked a little rigidly, but his arms swung loose by his sides, his air both jaunty and majestic, as he led me into his wood-paneled office—large enough to accommodate his old prison cell forty times over. The most urbane of hosts, he motioned me towards a set of chairs so finely upholstered that they would not have been out of place in the Palace of Versailles. Mandela, soon to turn seventy-six, was as gracefully at ease in his presidential role as if he had spent the past third of his life not in jail, but amidst the gilded trappings that his white predecessors had lavished on themselves to compensate for the indignity of knowing the rest of the world held them in contempt.

By a staggering turn of events, the man settling himself in his chair to face me had become quite possibly the most unanimously admired head of state in history. In truth, I was apprehensive. We'd met numerous times before. I had interviewed him; I had had plenty of chats with him, before and after press conferences and other public events since arriving in South Africa in January 1989, thirteen months before his release. Now, five and a half years later, on the morning of June 7, 1994, I felt intimidated. Before he had been a voteless freedom fighter, now he was an elected president. The great and the good had flocked from all over the world for his inauguration four weeks earlier here in these very Union Buildings, a vast brown pile perched on a hill above the South African capital that for eighty-four doleful years had been the seat of whites-only power. From this citadel, the apartheid laws had been enforced. From here, the chiefs of South Africa's dominant white tribe, the Afrikaners, administered a system that denied 85 percent of the population—those people born with dark skin—any say in the affairs of their country: They could not vote; they were sent to inferior schools so they could not compete with whites in the workplace; they were told where they could and could not live and what hospitals, buses, trains, parks, beaches, public toilets, public telephones they could and could not use.

Apartheid amounted, as Mandela once described it, to a moral genocide: an attempt to exterminate an entire people's self-respect. The United Nations called that "a crime against humanity," but the former masters of the Union Buildings believed that they were doing God's work on earth, and humanity be damned. With admirable logic, apartheid's Calvinist orthodoxy preached that black and white souls inhabited separate heavens, rendering it morally imperative for the chosen few to respond to those who rose in opposition to God's will with all the might that God in his bounty had awarded them. The ordinary black foot soldiers who rebelled were terrorized into submission, beaten by the police, sometimes tortured, in some cases assassinated, very often jailed without charge. The high-profile leaders, like Mandela, were punished with banishment to a barren island off the south Atlantic coast.

But Mandela endured and now, at last, he had stormed and taken the citadel. He never gloated in that hour we spent together, never came close to it, but the truth was that he had defeated apartheid's God, had kicked the Afrikaner interpretation of Calvinist theology into the dustbin of history. The apartheid laws had been wiped off the books, democratic elections had taken place in his country for the first time and the party he led, the African National Congress, had won with two-thirds of the national vote. He was the chief now, the president on the hilltop. He had fulfilled his destiny and done so in classic style, playing the part of the hero who rebels against tyranny, endures prison with Spartan forbearance, rises again to liberate his chained people and, in a twist unique to Mandela, finally forgives and redeems his enemies. Little wonder the world regarded him as a giant. He, while never betraying any suggestion of arrogance or pomposity, was aware of the global esteem in which he was held. And he knew I knew.

He sensed that I was nervous, but didn't show it, for that would have been impolite. He was aware of the effect he had on people. Everyone felt overawed in his presence, but Mandela took no delight in that. He wanted to be liked as much as he wanted to be admired.

So, he did with me as he did with everyone else: he strove to put me at ease by reducing himself to my terrestrial level, sending me a message, coded but clear enough, that he was just another toiling mortal, as I was. First, by greeting me as warmly as he did and showing he remembered my name and then, when we were sitting down, throwing me slightly, but again in a flattering way, by saying: "I must apologize. I feel certain we have obliged you to work very hard these last weeks." In a distinctive mannerism of his, he held onto the "e" of the word "very," adding an extra beat for emphasis. "Ve-ery hard." He said it with cheery mischief in his eye and I thought, as I had done the very first time I had seen him close up, on the morning after he left prison, how regal yet how approachable he was.

I chuckled at his apology and replied in the same spirit,

"Not as hard as you have been working, Mr. Mandela, I am sure."

"Ah, yes," he shot back, the smile widening, "but you were not loafing on an island for many years, as I was."

I laughed out loud. Self-deprecation was another of the ploys he used in the attempt to undercut the uneasy awe that he inspired. There was a British quality to that. I always thought Mandela, in another life, would have made a perfect chairman of one of those Victorian-era gentlemen's clubs that still exist in London. Very proper and correct, but superbly comfortable in his own skin. The impression was not accidental, for he had been taught by British missionaries as a child and, at the age of fourteen, as he would confess later, he knew more about the history of Britain, the battles of Hastings, Waterloo, and Trafalgar than he did about the Afrikaners' conquest of the southern tip of Africa or the wars of his own Xhosa tribe. When he was born his family named him Rohlihlahla, which means "tree-shaker" or "troublemaker" in Xhosa; it was a teacher at school who later gave him the name Nelson, in honor of the British Empire's most celebrated admiral.

Self-deprecation, as every Englishman since the time of Lord Nelson and before knows, is a subtle sport. There's a bogus element to it. In making light of your own achievements you are also, by a happy whim, drawing attention to them. There was more than a dash of vanity behind the claim that he had been loafing on Robben Island, for we both knew prison had been no Bahamas vacation. I picked up on that hint of weakness, his need to preen, and in a way he might not necessarily have meant, that served his purpose, too. It humanized him more in my eyes. Whatever the case, the magic, intended or unintended, worked—I had been put at my ease. Not on a footing of social equality, exactly, but sufficiently to be able to set about the business at hand with the composure not to make a fool of myself.

I switched on my cassette recorder and the interview began. I launched into my first political question, and as I uttered my first words his face changed, his smile vanished, his features turned to stone. It was always the way with Mandela. As soon as the subject turned serious, as soon as conversation turned to his life's mission, he listened with rapt, frozen concentration, his entire body stock-still. No more jokes now. But, happily, plenty of news.

He would leave office, he announced, after just one five-year presidential term. That was a bombshell right there. There had been suggestions in previous days that he would not be seeking re-election, but that was the first time he had publicly spelled out his intentions. It was quite a statement—a message to his country, his continent, and the world, an example to leaders everywhere who, whether popularly elected or after seizing power, all too often undermined the democracy they purported to uphold by succumbing to the vanity of imagining they were irreplaceable. Aware, rather, of his limitations, Mandela knew that come 1999, age would circumscribe his ability to do his job efficiently and he understood, too, that his talents lay not so much in day-to-day governance as in the symbolic consolidation of his country's new-found unity. He would play the role more of a nation-binding monarch than of a hands-on administrator.

That was why he also told me that much remained to be done to make sure all the good work of the liberation struggle was not undone. Segments of the far right remained armed and restless, unhappy with their government's decision to hand over power to the majority without a fight. Cementing the foundations of South Africa's inevitably fragile new democracy, he said, would be his principal challenge in office. I noted, a little quizzically, that the old apartheid coat of arms with its spectacularly ironic motto—"Ex Unitate Vires" (Out of Unity Strength)—remained on his office wall. Mandela replied that this would go soon enough, but that his government would move gingerly on the renaming of streets, towns, and public monuments, avoiding what might have been the revolutionist's temptation to trample on his defeated white compatriots' symbols of identity and pride.

It was rich, strong journalistic material, yet as I reflect on that interview now, nearly twenty years later, it is not so much what he said that has endured most in my memory, but the brief gesture, ten minutes into the interview, when there was a knock at the door and a middle-aged white woman entered the presidential office carrying a tray of tea.

Mandela, on seeing her, interrupted himself in midsentence and rose to his feet: There was a lady in the room. He greeted her effusively. "Ah, hello, Mrs. Coetzee! How are you?" He stood bolt upright while she fussed about, placing the cups, milk, and sugar on the table, and then a bottle of water and an empty glass. Then he introduced me to her. "Mrs. Coetzee, this is Mr. Carlin." I stood up—disgracefully, I had not done so. Then, the two of us shook hands. Mandela thanked her profusely for the tea, which was for me, and for the water, which she poured out for him. He did not sit down until Mrs. Coetzee left the room.

There had been a time, long before he went to prison, at the first law firm where he worked in the 1940s, when Mandela had been reprimanded by his white boss for drinking his tea from the same cups as the white employees. Mandela, who would later set up his own legal practice, had just arrived at the firm and had not understood that the tin cups were for the black workers, the porcelain ones for the white. But that indignity, together with the far greater ones he would endure later, had been forgotten now.

Mrs. Coetzee, whose name was classically Afrikaans, would have remembered those times. It was probable that, until quite recently, she had been responsible for administering the tea cup variation of "petty apartheid," as they used to call it, here at her place of work. For, as I suspected when I saw her enter Mandela's office (and would confirm later), she had been employed at the Union Buildings for some time. She had worked for Mandela's two predecessors, F. W. de Klerk, South Africa's last president, and P. W. Botha, a curmudgeon and a bully known by friends and foes as "the Big Crocodile." Mrs. Coetzee had been, in short, a loyal servant of the apartheid state. It would have been natural for Mandela to regard her as one more accomplice in the crime against humanity and to have treated her accordingly on becoming president by showing her the door.

And yet here he was, and here she was too. Not a glimmer of a grudge. He was all chivalry to this woman who would return the compliment a few days later by telling the local press that she had never been shown anything resembling Mandela's respect and kindness by the Afrikaner kin under whom she had worked before.

The curious thing was that, rather than bask in his own munificence, Mandela marveled at Mrs. Coetzee. He had bestowed on her the gift of forgiveness but, as he saw it, she had been generous to accept it. Alluding to her directly, a half hour after she left the room, it emerged that he was as taken in his own way with her as she had been with him. I asked him whether, despite the troubling undercurrents of unrest among the white right, he was surprised at the degree to which ordinary white people appeared to have adapted to the political changes. He was excited by the question.

"You know, that is perfectly true," he said. "Yes. Look at the lady who brought in the tea. Look at this! It is really unbelievable, the way they have just adjusted to the new position." It didn't seem to have occurred to him that she had adjusted in part because of the decency he had shown her. He had another explanation, a more practical one. "I think it is people, the nature of the human being," he said. "People want peace. They want security for themselves and for their children."

That was as true as it was manifestly wise, yet there was a part of the picture missing: his own part. Mandela made it plain that he never thought of himself as a god or even, as he said, as a saint. He knew his personal failings, and he knew that random factors over which he had no control played a part in obtaining his people's freedom. For example, what might have become of South Africa had P. W. Botha not suffered a stroke before Mandela's release, in 1989, forcing him to make way for the more pliable de Klerk? Nobody knows. Not even Mandela. Whether out of false or genuine modesty, he showed no inclination to claim the large part of the credit that was his due in winning over Mrs. Coetzee and, in time, the totality of the white population. Right then, at the very moment when I was interviewing him, he was at the peak of his life's achievements, yet power did not seem to have gone to his head. He was, as George Washington had been at the birth of the United States, his country's indispensable man. Many others had endured heavy sacrifices or had contributed their share of generosity and wisdom, but Mandela had been the chief architect of South Africa's peaceful revolution. Without him, as the turbulent priest of black liberation Archbishop Desmond Tutu once said to me, it simply would not have been possible.

It was his integrity and courage, allied to his powers of charm and persuasion, that had convinced his enemies to cede power voluntarily in the belief that he was a leader whom they could trust to forgo the path of revenge that their guilty consciences feared.

Mandela achieved that goal and many more, overcoming one seemingly impossible challenge after another, because, like Ulysses, whose feats of legend he would emulate within the less fantastic limits of the real world, he was as clever as he was virtuous, as cunning as he was bold. The story of Nelson Mandela in the years after his liberation is of triumph hard won. It tells how he conquered the serious press, domestic and foreign; how he conquered his own personal demons and his doubting, vengeful black followers; how he conquered the apartheid government and the warlike far right; how he conquered the people who worked alongside him after he became president and, finally, how, in one memorable action, he bonded his black and white compatriots to a degree otherwise unimaginable during the three-and-a-half centuries that followed the arrival of the first white settlers on the southern tip of Africa.

2

# GREAT EXPECTATIONS

**M**andela walking out of prison on Sunday, February 11, 1990, with his fist in the air is one of the twentieth century's most memorable images. We remember it as an occasion charged with political meaning, for it marked the beginning of the end of one of the world's most abominated tyrannies. What people may forget now is that it also satisfied, at the time, a tremendous curiosity. Mandela had been the world's most famous prisoner for a decade, but the world had no idea what he looked like, much less what sort of a person he might be. Photographers had been camped outside his prison near Cape Town for months prior to his release, unsure whether the government might spirit him out one day without warning. But the photographers had a problem: should he suddenly be released they had no idea how they would recognize him. One of them asked a white prison guard for guidance. The guard replied, "Don't worry. When you see him you'll know exactly who he is. There's no one like him."

The guard was right. Lean, tall, and radiant in a tailored

*11*

gray suit and elegant blue tie, Mandela emerged from prison into the bright afternoon sunlight looking every inch a king.

Yet all was not what it seemed on that historic day. While black South Africa and most of the world celebrated, there was much anxious brooding behind the scenes. Those in the apartheid government who had set him free and those from his own side, in the African National Congress, both feared, in very different ways, that in Mandela they might have unleashed a force neither would be able to control. The perception among the political classes now was that Mandela's release would ease in a new era of negotiations which would abolish apartheid and establish a new democratic order. No one was in any doubt that the process would be, in the best of circumstances, arduous and delicate. At the upper levels of both the government and the ANC, there was a concern that Mandela might destabilize the whole enterprise before it even began.

My own worry at the time, widely shared I believe, was whether Mandela the man would live up to Mandela the myth. Or would he turn out to be a terrible letdown? By the end of his first day as a free man, I was not so sure what the answer was. Seeing him had been one thing; hearing him talk several hours later was another. His first speech as a free man was a dull disappointment, as was much of the rest of what followed the first glimpse of his release from prison.

Of the hundreds of millions of people watching that moment live on television, the great majority probably chose to savor that glimpse. The Free Nelson Mandela campaign had grown into a worldwide clamor over the previous decade— it was practically the only political cause on which the planet was not divided during the Cold War. When the global audience saw him step out a free man, one may suppose that those present would have responded as the script required: applauding, smiling, shedding tears, and raising glasses in Mandela's name. Given the day's historical significance, they would have been right to do so.

For those of us who were covering the event up close in the southern tip of the African continent that Francis Drake described as "the fairest cape," the reality was less than glorious. Take away that magical first minute during which a beaming Mandela and his formidable wife, Winnie, marched hand in hand out of the prison gate, and the truth was that it was a gigantic flop. Chaotic, too. Mandela had been scheduled to end the day with a press conference before the hordes of newspeople from all over the world assembled in Cape Town, but everything had been delayed due to the incapacity of Mandela's people to control some of their followers, and the government's inability to restrain the brutal impulses of the police. The press conference had to be postponed until the next morning, adding fuel to the prejudices of unsympathetic observers who had long joked that the African National Congress, far from being prepared either to negotiate or to govern, "could not run a bath."

First, Mandela's actual release took place two hours later than scheduled because his wife Winnie, "the Mother of the Nation," had flown down late from Johannesburg to Cape Town, half an hour's drive from the prison. (According to a government minister to whom I spoke much later, she was delayed at the hairdresser's.) Second, his speech at Cape Town's biggest square, the Grand Parade, took place not at three, as originally anticipated, but five hours later, when dusk had fallen. Young black looters, ostensibly ANC supporters, and trigger-happy white policemen had reduced the place to a shambles, raising fears for Mandela's safety. No sooner had Mandela emerged from prison than he was whisked into a car and removed from public view. For several hours, the press had no idea where he was. It turned out that his convoy had been hiding on a backstreet in what remained a whites-only Cape Town suburb, waiting for the danger to pass. I learned later that Mandela rolled down his window to greet a mightily surprised young white couple walking in the neighborhood with their twin babies. Fortunately, they were a liberal-minded pair who happily acceded to Mandela's request that they pass their children through the car window for him to hug.

When he finally made it to the Grand Parade for his speech, the big square contained about 40 percent fewer people than had filled it in midafternoon. The violence on the periphery of the square, the blistering midsummer heat, or simply the need to attend to household matters had persuaded many of his followers and curious onlookers to skip their date with history and follow the climax of the day's proceedings on television.

They didn't miss much. Looking older in metal-framed glasses than he had when he emerged out of the prison gates, he read from a prepared text. Maybe it was the gathering evening gloom and the relative flatness of the public mood, or perhaps it was simply that the day's dramas had drained his energy. Perhaps it was the lifelessness of most of the words he read, a shopping list of predictable political demands and tired slogans. Whatever the case, it was not an uplifting speech. He even provided a headline for those hungry to portray him as an unreconstructed terrorist by declaring that "the armed struggle" would continue.

The truth was that there was little armed struggle to speak of: the ANC were the most unconvincing, halfhearted guerrilla movement on the face of the earth. I spent six years in Central America prior to arriving in South Africa and witnessed firsthand the military operations of, among others, the guerrillas of El Salvador, whose inferiority of numbers against a U.S.-trained army had not stopped them from regularly overrunning military garrisons, displaying stealth, courage, and discipline reminiscent of the Viet Cong. The ANC's armed wing, which grandly called themselves Umkhonto we Sizwe, meaning "Spear of the Nation," might have had a fair amount of mettle, but were largely ineffectual. They did set off the odd bomb, but were so thoroughly infiltrated by the South African security police and military intelligence that the apartheid authorities often knew more about their invariably frustrated operations than the exiled leadership of the ANC did.

Mandela also spoke about nationalizing the gold and diamond mines, the chief source of South Africa's wealth. That sent a shiver up the spines of white businessmen, fearful that Mandela was a closet Red. Any serious political analyst knew that, in light of the recent fall of the Berlin Wall and the collapse of communism generally, any suggestion of implementing economic policies of that sort was sheer bluster, with no practical purpose beyond perhaps keeping the fire of rebellion simmering among the ANC faithful.

A bit of Martin Luther King brio might have livened up proceedings but oratory, it became immediately and heart-sinkingly apparent, was not Mandela's forte. Not, at any rate, when his speeches had been written for him. He spoke in a metallic monotone, rarely striking an emotional chord. No rousing iterations, no dramatic pauses, barely any gesticulation. Archbishop Tutu, himself a sparkling orator, would in time become very close to Mandela but, as he gently put it to me once, "I wouldn't say Mandela was a man to set the Thames alight with his speeches."

In fairness, Mandela did offer one rhetorical pearl on that night of his release: "I stand here before you," he declared, "not as a prophet but as a humble servant of you, the people." But the impact was lost, or at any rate diluted, in the drabness of the delivery. The last speech he had given had been in

1964 when he was on trial, facing the death penalty. The final flourish of that speech had made it into a hundred literary anthologies. "I have fought against white domination and I have fought against black domination," he had said. "I have cherished the ideal of a democratic and free society in which all persons live together in harmony and with equal opportunities. It is an ideal which I hope to live for and to achieve. But if needs be, it is an ideal for which I am prepared to die."

The best Mandela could do now, on this historic day of his liberation, was to end his speech quoting those very words from so many years ago. And fine words they were, but it was a surprise that he had not been able to come up with something grander, or more fitting to the occasion. My first utterly depressing thought was that his best days must surely lie behind him. My second reflection was that his speech had been written by ANC apparatchiks under orders to dim his messiah light.

Whether that had been the intention or not, the speech was a disappointment to all but the ANC leadership—and, as it happened, to the white government. For me, and for many of the other journalists on the scene, the contrast between the expectations Mandela had generated and the deflating reality of his first words had been disheartening. But the leaders of the liberation movement were content enough. They had been fretting for months over the possibility that Mandela, who inside prison had been engaging in secret talks with the government without the ANC's knowledge, might have a political agenda of his own or, worse, that his mind was failing him. Some were suspicious. Had Mandela become a government pawn? Were the apartheid schemers planning to use him to divide the ANC? Had the ANC erred in building his reputation to such a great height, identifying him in black South African minds as the incarnation of their freedom struggle? Or, in a nightmare scenario that some contemplated, had he been guilefully manipulated into becoming apartheid's Trojan horse? The power of his word was such, the ANC knew, that whatever he said upon his release, whatever orders he gave, they would be followed. That speech, that text, was the liberation movement showing its collective muscle, seeking to rein in the old man.

The relief of the government was, if anything, greater. The ruling National Party feared, upon releasing Mandela, that far from having lured him into a trap, he might have taken them for a ride—that his sweet words of reconciliation in the three years of talks they had conducted with him had been just that: words. They feared what the chief of South African intelligence, Niel Barnard, would later describe to me as "the Ayatollah Factor." In other words, as Ayatollah Khomeini did upon his return to Iran from exile, Mandela would exhort his supporters to raze the old order to the ground and drive the whites—in a phrase popular among the wilder black militants at the time—into the sea. That was patently not his message during that first speech, and Barnard and the others in government who had made the decision to release Mandela went to bed that night, as did the ANC leadership, in a calmer state of mind than they had done twenty-four hours earlier.

I didn't. I ended that historic day, as many others did, with misgivings, wondering whether Mandela would fail to live up to the world's expectations. He would in all likelihood reveal himself to be a decent old fellow, but, at seventy-one, would he not turn out to be sadly out of touch? A lot had changed politically during his imprisonment, both within South Africa and abroad. In his absence, a new generation of young black political activists had emerged, forged in street battles with the police more violent than any Mandela had known. The fall of the Berlin Wall had altered the ideological landscape on which he had fought his old political struggles. When he had gone to prison, television had not yet come to South Africa. The probability seemed to be, in short, that he would be too old, too confused, too removed from the realities of the modern world to put his stamp on his country's politics. And now, the day after his release, his qualities of leadership would have to withstand the scrutiny of a press conference at which some of the world's most experienced and hard-nosed journalists would interrogate him on his policies and plans. Would it turn out to be a fiasco?

I worried about all this because, in truth, I was no more objective a journalist during my first year in South Africa than I would have been had I been doing the same job in Berlin in 1936. Black South Africans all around the country had been celebrating Mandela's release as if their own day of freedom had come, or at least as if it were just around the corner. I wanted to believe that they were right. White South Africans were worried that, in the best of cases, it was the end of the giant and outrageous affirmative action program apartheid had created for their benefit and, in the worst, that the nightmare of vengeful black mobs storming their homes, would finally come to pass.

Yet, the events of the previous day suggested that both black hopes and white fears would be unfounded. In the political battle that lay ahead between Mandela and President F. W. de Klerk, and between Mandela's ANC and de Klerk's National Party, apartheid's inventors and enforcers, everything seemed to indicate that the bad guys would run rings around the good. The ANC were almost as much of an unknown entity to the South African population as Mandela was, having been declared illegal, or "banned," in 1960. They went underground, remaining in the shadows, their leadership in exile, until the unbanning by de Klerk just nine days before Mandela's release.

The press conference was rescheduled for seven a.m. the morning of Monday, February 12, the day after his liberation. The venue was the impeccably tended garden at the official residence of Desmond Tutu, who, as well as being the Anglican archbishop of South Africa, had won the Nobel Peace Prize in 1984 for his brave and outspoken opposition to apartheid. A gabled white mansion in the Dutch colonial style, Tutu's home sat on the foothills of Table Mountain, a vast slab of rock overlooking Cape Town, whose shadow Mandela had peered at across the sea during his eighteen years on Robben Island. The sun shone, but the air was crisp and dew still hung on the flowers as Nelson and Winnie Mandela made their entrance, strolling out of the house and onto a lawn where a row of chairs and a long table, crowded with microphones, awaited them. Some two hundred journalists from all over the world craned their necks, studying the famous couple's every gesture, following their every step. The image that stays in my mind is of a king and queen in the final scene of a Shakespearean garden production, giving their serene blessing to a healing marriage ceremony. But the dread that he would turn out to be a confused old-timer returned when he touched a microphone and was heard to say, "What is this?"

Winnie sat at his right. She had supported Mandela's cause stoically during the last years of his incarceration, sometimes, (more often than Mandela would have liked) with violent fervor. Yet, to the surprise of those of us who knew her, she played the demure bride, resisting any urge she might have had to seize the spotlight and venture some opinions of her own. On Mandela's left, also silent, was Walter Sisulu, his best friend and closest political ally, the man who had recruited him to the cause of black liberation nearly fifty years earlier, and who had spent more than half that time in prison with him, locked up in a nearby cell. They were there for moral support. As it turned out, Mandela did not need it.

His larger mission today was to reach out to South Africa and the world, but his immediate task was to win over the audience before him. As we began to discover, he had not been as out of touch with political events as some of us had imagined. An avid consumer of news during his last years in prison, when it later emerged that earlier restrictions on his access to the press had been lifted, he had in fact acquired as sharp an understanding as any modern politician of the importance of getting the media messengers on your side. He began, as he would with me at that interview in the Union Buildings years later, by flattering our collective vanity, boosting our often fragile self-esteem. His response to the very first question, about how he felt in his first morning as a free man, was exquisitely calculated. At the time it did not occur to me to ponder whether he was genuine or putting on an act. I was simply charmed, as I am certain most of my colleagues were, too.

"First," he said, "I think it proper for us to apologize for the failure to hold the press conference yesterday and we very much regret we could not fulfill that commitment." That old-fashioned word "proper," which I would hear over and over from him in the coming years, and the unnecessarily solemn accompanying phrase "fulfill that commitment" brought a touch of distinction to the apology, and with it an engaging suggestion of naivety, rendering it all the more sincere to our captive ears.

"I am absolutely excited at getting out and I am also excited to have the opportunity of addressing you because throughout these difficult years in prison the press, both local and foreign, has been a brick to us. I think it was the original intention of the government that we should be forgotten. It was the press that kept the memory of those who have been imprisoned for offenses they committed in the course of their political activities; it was the press who never forgot us and we are therefore indebted to you. I am happy to be with you this morning."

The press conference lasted forty minutes, and was an exercise in seduction from start to finish. At the time we had no idea how artfully we were being manipulated. Those of us who asked questions had to identify ourselves by our names and by the news media we represented. He was especially attentive to the half dozen South African reporters who asked questions, almost all of whom belonged to what ANC dogma regarded as the enemy camp. To one from the chief arm of state propaganda and disinformation, the South African Broadcasting Corporation, he responded with a cheery, "Ah, hello! How are you?" To another from a newspaper associated with white free enterprise, "Hi! I am happy to see you!" To a political writer from an Afrikaans newspaper, "Good to see you!" To another Afrikaans journalist whose name he recognized from his own reading of the newspapers, "Ah, yes! But I was expecting you to be a little taller and stouter!"

Just as we had expected him to be a little frailer, but he seemed as healthy in body as lively in mind. I'd confirm the impression a few weeks later when, to my amazement and delight, his personal doctor agreed to see me. In what may have been a mild violation of his Hippocratic Oath, he told me that prison had not done Mandela's constitution much harm at all; in fact, the fresh air, the regular diet, the unstressed routine of life, and even the forced labor had done him much good. The doctor, an Afrikaner, said Mandela had emerged from prison, at seventy-one, in the physical shape of a very fit man of fifty.

Was he fit to engage in the protracted political battle with the white state that lay ahead? Did he have his wits about him sufficiently to engineer the peaceful overthrow of apartheid? Mandela answered these questions swiftly enough. Behind all

the hearty banter with the journalists, once he had dispensed
with the courtesies, we found there was plenty of substance,
too. His broader purpose was, through the press, to reach out
to his complex and deeply divided South African audience,
taking his first steps on a journey whose final objective, wildly
overambitious at the time, was to brook the racial, political
and historical divisions and win the trust of all his compatriots. Equally important, though, he had to secure his own
internal flank, and appease the doubters within the ANC.

He spoke to this end in the first person plural, being quick
to stress early on, "We are loyal and disciplined members of the
organization," and showing it by proclaiming his adherence to
such ANC articles of faith as the maintenance of international
sanctions against the régime. Asked why he persisted with the
option of armed struggle now that he was free, he gladdened
ANC hearts when he judiciously replied, "I have committed
myself to the promotion of peace in this country. . . . The
armed struggle is merely defensive, a defensive act against the
violence of apartheid."

The point was simply articulated, as befitted a man who
had trained as a lawyer before turning his sights to revolution, but in a manner more succinctly compelling than I had
ever heard from any other apologist for guerrilla action. The
problem was that the term "armed struggle" made the hairs
of white South Africans stand on end. Keenly aware that his
most difficult and decisive mission on reentering political
life was to persuade the government to give up power without a fight, he had concluded after long deliberation in prison
that he had erred in imagining apartheid would be overcome
through force of arms. The road lay through persuading the
white population that he was not a terrorist bent on vengeance,
but a leader they could rely on.

This was his answer when I asked him whether, given

de Klerk's known desire for a new political order that would somehow award whites a disproportionate voice in the affairs of state, he saw any room for accommodation between the ANC and the government. "The ANC is very much concerned to address the question of the concerns of whites," he replied. "Over the demand of one-person-one-vote, they are concerned that the realization of this demand does not result in domination of whites by blacks. We understand those fears and the ANC is concerned to address the problem and to find a solution that will suit both the blacks and the whites of this country."

Not many whites would have taken his good intentions at face value but among some, at least, he would have sown some helpful seeds of doubt. The man who sat here talking so soberly, yet so sunnily, bore little resemblance to the fearsome black avenger portrayed by the apartheid propaganda machine. He bore little resemblance, for that matter, to the angry freedom fighter he had been when he was arrested and imprisoned in August 1962, the rebel who had founded Umkhonto we Sizwe and, as its commander in chief, had consciously modeled himself, right down to the beard and the camouflage jacket, on the revolutionary heroes of the age: Fidel Castro and Che Guevara. Prison reminded him that success in politics requires an accurate measure of the limits of what's possible. Prison mellowed his militancy but sharpened his vision. He came quickly to understand that the notion of "taking power the Castro way," as an ANC slogan of the time had it, was little more than a dream. Or that, in the best of cases, a long guerrilla war of attrition would yield, in the end, what he would later call "the peace of the cemeteries." Given the might of the South African police and military, a Cuban-style armed insurrection was not a plausible outcome. The transfer of power, when it came, would have to come through negotiations. Armed struggle was useful and, indeed, necessary, Mandela judged, as a bargaining tool in negotiations and as a means of imbuing the black population, demoralized by his arrest, with the dignity of feeling that they were fighting back. But that was all. In a candid moment, one of the ANC's more clear-sighted leaders had acknowledged not long before Mandela's release that "armed struggle" might more accurately be called "armed propaganda."

When the time came, and now that Mandela was finally free it would come soon, formally abandoning the armed struggle would be a useful bone to toss President de Klerk. Mandela made it clear in that first press conference that he had a mature understanding of negotiations as a two-way street: on the one hand, you would be trying to get the better of your political rivals; on the other, both sides would end up in a form of partnership, bonded by the common goal of reaching what would inevitably have to be a compromise. In that spirit, Mandela surprised those of us present, and the world at large, by describing de Klerk, a long time apartheid advocate who had been in parliament since 1969 and occupied ministerial position in government for eleven years before becoming president of South Africa in 1989, as "a man of integrity." Neither did Mandela hesitate to spell out that he understood the need for the ANC to offer gestures in due course that would help de Klerk "carry the National Party with him" throughout the transition. In other words, in anticipation of the political process that would unfold, he saw that de Klerk would struggle to sell the concessions he would have to make to the white constituency. He would need Mandela's help and, if Mandela judged him deserving, he would give it.

Mandela was in fact helping de Klerk already, and serving his own long-term ends by emphasizing repeatedly in the press conference his sensitivity to white anxieties. There was no notion of blacks doing to whites as whites had done to blacks.

"Whites are fellow South Africans," he said, "and we want them to feel safe, to know that we appreciate the contribution they have made towards the development of this country." It was a staggeringly generous statement to make of a people who, since the arrival of the first Dutch settlers in 1652, had treated the black indigenous population as second-class citizens or outright slaves. But there was much more to it than an expression of human kindness. Mandela revealed himself to us as a cold-eyed pragmatist, as a chess player always five moves ahead of his opponent.

He was presented with an opportunity at the press conference that others in his place might have seized to ventilate some resentment. Did he harbor any regrets or bitterness after being confined to prison for twenty-seven years? In his response, he did offer a glimpse of the suffering he had endured, but it was the political animal that prevailed. Whether Winnie Mandela had different feelings, the white South African state having shown little mercy to her or their two daughters, we had no way of knowing. She sat poker-faced as Mandela launched into his reply.

"I have lost a great deal over these twenty-seven years. My wife has been under all sorts of pressures and it is not a nice feeling for a man to see his family struggling without security, without dignity, without the head of the family around. But despite the hard time we have had in prison we have also had the opportunity to think about problems, and it is an opportunity which is also very rewarding in that regard. And you learn to get used to your circumstances. In prison there have been men who were very good in the sense that they understood our point of view and did everything to try and make you as happy as possible. And that has wiped out any bitterness that a man may have."

Prison had taught him to take the long view and preserve

his self-control. He glossed over the pressures his wife and family had faced because that was terrain which risked undermining the upbeat mood he was striving to convey on his reentry into public life. But nice it definitely had not been, for his family or for him, helpless in prison to come to their aid. The men he chose to acknowledge were his jailers, politically unsophisticated, instinctively racist Afrikaners when Mandela first met them, who softened under his spell and with whom, as I would discover, he forged in some cases astonishingly close relationships. As to his lack of bitterness, the attribute in Mandela most often highlighted by foreign commentators, he no doubt did feel that way in the elation of his release, at least in part. But the price his family paid had been high, including constant harassment by police and spells in prison for his wife. The truth was that the consequences of his absence as a husband and father would always haunt him.

Declaring that all bitterness had been erased was not so much the impulse of a saint, but the most striking example of Mandela's ability to bury his feelings in the interests of his political goals. It was the most persuasive way of conveying to the white population that they were not to worry; revenge was not on his agenda.

The message was intended for his own supporters, too. During the year I lived in South Africa, the activists I encountered had been, in many cases, young and impulsive, prey to revolutionary posturing, ensnared in the fantasies of armed insurrection. Mandela's performance at the press conference was a statement to them and to South Africa that a mature patriarch had taken charge and the time for rash action and dangerous talk from his followers was over. But would he measure up against white South Africa's other leaders? Mandela had a seemingly formidable opponent in the experienced and sophisticated President de Klerk, who might only have been elected by a tenth of his country's population, but he had stolen the headlines in previous months, winning his régime an unheard of measure of global acceptance with initiatives that had opened up the political playing field like never before.

De Klerk, whom I had studied closely for nearly a year, was the most effective public relations advocate the apartheid government had ever seen, and the most reformist, too. But the fresh evidence before my eyes told me that where de Klerk, also a lawyer, was the back-room attorney, Mandela was the commanding courtroom performer. Where de Klerk was clever and well-mannered, Mandela was wise and magisterial. De Klerk knew how to smile for the cameras; Mandela had a natural smile, a natural glamour, a natural gravitas. De Klerk was an accidental hero; Mandela was a man of destiny. De Klerk had star quality, but he belonged to a lesser constellation.

Unlike de Klerk, a practiced modern politician, Mandela had never held a formal press conference. He had faced a TV camera only once, in a clandestine interview with one reporter, just before going to prison. Suddenly, he was being confronted by thirty cameras and two hundred reporters. Yet, his aplomb was absolute. He sat before us as if he were with old friends. Before a large gathering, reading a speech from a distant podium, he had come across as a stern schoolmaster. His talent for communication, it became evident, lay in the close encounter, which was—uncannily—how that press conference, fewer than twenty-four hours after his release into the wide world, felt. He answered each question with courteous ease and measured clarity of purpose but also with the evasive caution of an expert politician, while contriving never to elicit the suspicion that he was being economical with the truth.

With so much delicacy that we barely noticed it, Mandela had planted his fist on the table. In a manner I had not anticipated after hearing his speech the day before, he had left no doubt that from now on he would occupy center stage on the national landscape. As his exultant host, Desmond Tutu, put it to me later, "You feared that he would emerge with, so to speak, feet of clay. But what a wonder! What a hallelujah! That he should have been everything that we had imagined and more! And that his message should have been, 'Let's try reconciliation,' when the crazies could have replied, 'What, you? You talking so glibly about forgiving, what do you know about our suffering?' But of course he had suffered so much more than they had, he had the credibility of his twenty-seven years in prison behind him and so they had no answer. He was the one in charge."

Mandela had been more in charge during his last years in prison than anyone had known. He would now take charge openly, for all to see. Dashing all doubts, his first press conference as a free man was a tour de force, a master class in political persuasion. This was Mandela playing himself, not operating from any script. It was Mandela unbound and the ANC gained more from his liberation than the skeptics within would ever have imagined. He was not a fanatic. He was not even a romantic. He was a hard-nosed pragmatist who inspired admiration, even among the most inveterate skeptics. When the press conference was over, something happened that I had never seen before or have ever seen again in 30 years reporting on politicians. Hypnotizing us into forgetting we were working journalists, making a mockery of our pretensions to objectivity, he drew from us a long burst of spontaneous, heartfelt applause.

# 3

# NELSON AND CLEOPATRA

Two weeks before Mandela's release, I went to see his wife, Winnie, at her home in Soweto. President de Klerk had not yet made the official announcement, but we knew he would be out soon. She lived in Diepkloof Extension, the posh neighborhood of South Africa's most famous segregated black township, on the edge of South Africa's biggest city, Johannesburg. Beverly Hills was how the area was known to Soweto residents, many of whose two million inhabitants dwelled in replicas of the small home that Winnie and her husband had shared with their two small daughters and his frail mother before he went to prison: two-bedroom boxes of dark red brick built one next to the other in dense, neat rows as far as the eye could see. That was the township model devised by apartheid's diligent municipal engineers, and re-created in every urban area where black South Africans lived. Diepkloof Extension was a private initiative, where the handful of black people who had contrived to make a little money resided. Winnie's home, funded by foreign benefactors, was a two-floor, three-bedroom house with a garden and a small swimming pool. The height of ex-

travagance by black standards, in those days it would have
more or less met the aspirations of the average white, middle-
class South African.

Zindzi, Winnie's slim and attractive second daughter, was
twenty-nine, but looked younger in yellow t-shirt and denim
dungarees. Usually, when I visited black people's homes in
Soweto and elsewhere there was an awkwardness in the first
encounter. Unfailingly, I was invited to come in, sit down, and
have a cup of tea. But it did take people a little while to get over
the surprise of seeing a white man under their own roof in a
country where 98 percent of the white population had never
set foot in a black township.

With Zindzi there was no awkwardness at all. It was nine-
thirty in the morning and she was in the kitchen frying eggs.
She invited me in and started chatting as if we were old friends.
"Mum," she said, was still upstairs and would probably be a
while. The truth was that I had not scheduled an interview
with Winnie. I had just dropped in to try my luck. Zindzi
knew it, I think, but took no offense. She was worldly enough
to know that this was a good moment for a journalist to get
an interview with her mother and saw nothing wrong in me
giving it a shot. As I hovered about waiting (and, as it turned
out, waiting, and waiting), friends of Zindzi's wandered in for
coffee and a chat. Completing the South African middle-class
picture, a small, wizened maid in blue overalls padded inscru-
tably around the place, clearing cups and washing dishes.

Finally, Winnie made her entrance. Taller than I had expected, very much the grand-dame, she displayed neither
surprise nor irritation at my presence in her home. When I
said I would like to interview her she responded with a sigh,
a knowing smile (journalists had been chasing her all her
life), and a glance at her watch. I said all I'd need was half an
hour. She thought a moment, shrugged her shoulders and said,

"Okay. But you will have to give me a little time." She still had to put the finishing touches to her morning toilette.

The picture presented me by mother, daughter, friends, and cleaning lady was of a domesticity so stable and relaxed that, had I not been better informed, I would never have imagined the depths of trauma that lurked beneath. Winnie had been continually harassed and persecuted by agents of the apartheid state during the seventies and eighties; she had borne the anguish of hearing her two small daughters screaming as the police broke into her home and carted her off to jail; she had spent more than a year in solitary confinement in a cell, trusting that her confused and stricken children would be cared for by friends; she had been banished and placed under house arrest in a lost township in the Orange Free State, far away from her Soweto home.

But she was back, her circumstances altered dramatically for the better now that Mandela's release was imminent. The authorities no longer saw any benefit in antagonizing the man with whom they had now resolved to do political business, and this meant leaving Winnie well alone, in peace to resume her marital role.

One hour after her first entrance, she majestically reappeared, Cleopatra in a satin African robe. But Cleopatra still needed her morning coffee, and motioned me to wait in her study while she withdrew into the kitchen. She returned five minutes later, time enough for me to take in the surroundings. On a wall there was a "Free Nelson Mandela" poster, a gift from the Anti-Apartheid Movement at 13 Mandela Street, London. Alongside it, another poster, in the green, yellow, and black colors of the African National Congress, at that point still an illegal organization. On a bookshelf there was a row of framed family portraits, a Christmas card and a birthday card. Only a month had passed since Christmas, but nearly six since Winnie had turned fifty-five. I could not resist taking a closer look. I opened the Christmas card, which was enormous, the size of a tabloid newspaper, and immediately recognized, from old documents I had seen, Mandela's large, spidery handwriting. "Darling, I love you. Madiba," it said. Madiba was the tribal name, affectionate and venerable at the same time, by which he liked to be known to those close to him. On the birthday card he had written the same words, under the manufacturer's standard endearment, "What a difference it makes in my life to have you!"

If I had not known better I might have imagined the cards had been sent by an infatuated teenager. Once we sat down and began our interview, Winnie took on just such a role, playing the tremulous bride-to-be, convincing me she was in a state of nervous excitement at the prospect of rekindling her life's great love. She showed me her other face, too, that of the disciplined freedom fighter, the woman who, in her husband's absence, had become South Africa's most visible symbol of black resistance. She had been out on the barricades, nose to nose with the riot police, but she was politically sharp, too. Mandela's imminent release would be "a new leaf in the history of South Africa," she said, but what direction the country would take after that was another matter. "We all equate his release with the dream we have cherished throughout the years—and there may be danger in that, to sort of imagine that with his release we will automatically solve the issues of the day," she told me. "The government has had to go a very long way to accept the reality of the South African situation."

Winnie's warning proved prophetic. Four and a half dangerous years would pass, with negotiations between the government and the ANC under continual threat from the violence of the far right, before white people began to make peace with the reality of majority rule.

Winnie left a lasting impression on me that morning. I had only seen her from a distance before, in one case formidably standing up to a white policeman and his teeth-bared Alsatian in the middle of a violent demonstration. Close up she had, like her husband, the charisma of the vastly self-confident, and there was a coquettish, eye-fluttering sensuality about her. It was not hard to imagine how the young woman who met Mandela one rainy evening in 1957 had struck him, as he would later confess, like a thunderbolt. Figuratively speaking, that is. Though I did read that in the course of the relentless harassment she endured from the police during her years alone, a white policeman had broken into her bedroom while she was getting dressed and, incensed, she had hurled him to the floor and broken his neck.

As for Mandela, she would end up breaking his heart. The Mandela the world saw wore a mask that disguised his private feelings, presenting himself as a fearless hero, immune to ordinary human weakness. His effectiveness as a leader hung, he believed, on keeping that public mask from cracking. She offered the greatest test to his resolve. During the years that I followed Mandela's footsteps the mask cracked—letting a glimmer of private sadness or regret—only twice. Winnie was the cause both times.

The first time was in May 1991. She had just been convicted at Johannesburg's Rand Supreme Court of assault and accessory to kidnapping, her victim a fourteen-year-old black boy called Stompie Moeketsi whom her driver had subsequently murdered. Winnie had been led to believe, falsely as it turned out, that the boy had been working as a spy for the apartheid state. Winnie and Mandela walked together down the steps of the grand court building. Once again the actress, she swaggered to the street to accept the cheers of a small group of diehard supporters wearing a broad smile on her face, right fist raised in triumph. It was not clear what she could possibly have been celebrating, except perhaps the perplexing fact that she had not been whisked straight off to jail and would remain free pending an appeal. Mandela had a different grasp of the situation. His face was gray; his eyes, downcast. Unable to ignore the enormity of the crime of which his wife had been convicted, he could not keep his feelings hidden. The judge's verdict had doused his public bonhomie.

The second and last time that Mandela stood before us, shorn of all possible pretense, visibly battling on this occasion to stop himself from breaking down, was nearly a year after Winnie's criminal conviction. The setting was an evening press conference hastily summoned at Shell House, the drab headquarters of the ANC in downtown Johannesburg. He shuffled into the cramped, airless room, his face fixed in an expression as grave as I would ever see him wear, as the cameras clicked madly away, capturing his sorrow for posterity.

There were no pleasantries this time—no cheery greetings or apologies for making us work late in the day. He sat down at a table before us, his oldest and most intimate friends Walter Sisulu and Oliver Tambo by his side, looking like pallbearers. Then he read from a piece of paper, beginning by paying tribute to his wife.

"During the two decades I spent on Robben Island she was an indispensable pillar of support and comfort to myself personally. She endured the persecutions heaped upon her by the government with exemplary fortitude and never wavered from her commitment to the struggle for freedom. Her tenacity reinforced my personal respect, love and growing affection. It also attracted the admiration of the world at large. My love for her remains undiminished."

There was a general intake of breath at that, for we all knew things were not well between them, but then he continued: "We have mutually agreed that a separation would be the best for each of us. . . . I part from my wife with no recriminations. I embrace her with all the love and affection I have nursed for her inside and outside prison from the moment I first met her."

He stopped reading and immediately rose to his feet. "Ladies and gentlemen, I hope you'll appreciate the pain I have gone through and I now end this interview."

In normal circumstances, had he been any other politician, at least four or five out of the hundred or so journalists present would have been unable to resist the impulse to shout a question. There was plenty we could have asked, such as what specifically had precipitated the separation, how long had it been in coming, when did he realize the marriage was over, or what would be the impact of his personal distress on an unfinished political quest. We all knew this would be the biggest news story in the world that day, but no one said a word. Even the photographers stopped clicking. He exited the room, head bowed, amidst total silence.

It was a tribute as eloquent in its way as the applause we had given him at the end of the first press conference after his release. He had appealed to our better natures and we had responded. To have intruded on his grief would have been the summit of insensitivity.

I remember asking myself at the time why he had put himself through this. He did not have to announce the end of his marriage in person. No one would have blamed him for releasing the news in the form of a statement. But he had always said that his life belonged not to himself, but to the nation. The only explanation I could find was that, when put most painfully to the test, he believed he should act in a manner consistent with that claim.

I heard from people who worked with him at ANC headquarters that for some weeks he withdrew into himself as he never had before and never would later. He fell into a dark mood, forsaking his usual easy banter, abandoning the habitual courtesies with his staff. Mandela's love for Winnie had been, like many great loves, a kind of madness, all the more so in his case as it was founded more on a fantasy that he had kept alive for twenty-seven years in prison than on the brief time they had actually spent together. On the face of it, they had lived under the same roof for four years; in reality the demands of his political life, which at that time often meant being on the run from the police, were such that they had next to no experience of married life, as Winnie herself would confess to me that morning in her home. "I have never lived with Mandela," she said. "I have never known what it was to have a close family where you sat around the table with husband and children. I have no such dear memories. When I gave birth to my children he was never there, even though he was not in jail at the time."

It seemed that Winnie, who was twenty-two years old to his thirty-eight when they met, had cast a spell on him. Or maybe he cast a spell on himself, needing to reconstruct those fleeting memories of her into a fantasy of tranquility where he sought refuge from the loneliness of prison life.

The truth was that Winnie had had several lovers during Mandela's long absence. The one she had been having an affair with during the last months before his release was a lawyer thirty years her junior and a member of her defense team in the previous year's trial, Dali Mpofu. She carried on with the affair after Mandela left prison. ANC members close to Mandela knew what was going on, as they did about her frequent bouts of drunkenness. I tried asking them why they didn't talk to Mandela about Winnie's waywardness, but I was always met by frosty stares. Winnie became a taboo subject within the ANC during those two years after Mandela left prison. What became clear to me then was that his impeccably courteous public persona acted as a coat of armor protecting the sorrowing man within. Confronting Mandela with the truth about Winnie was a step too far for the freedom fighters of the ANC. But there came a point when Mandela could deceive himself, or the public, no longer.

Details of the affair with Mpofu were made luridly public in a newspaper report two weeks before the separation announcement. There could be nothing more humiliating for a man than to see exposed the vulnerable core beneath the hard shell he sought to show the world. The article was a devastating, irrefutable exposé of Winnie's affair. It was based on a letter, published by the newspaper, that Winnie had written to Mpofu. It was the rant of a woman betrayed.

The letter revealed that Mpofu had recently had a child with a white woman whom she referred to as "a white hag" and accused him of "running around fucking at the slightest emotional excuse."

"Before I am through with you, you are going to learn a bit of honesty and sincerity and know what betrayal of one's love means to a woman," the letter said. "Remember always how much you have hurt and humiliated me . . . I keep telling you the situation is deteriorating at home, you are not bothered because you are satisfying yourself every night with a woman. I won't be your bloody fool, Dali."

It is hard to conceive how excruciating it would have been for a man as emotionally restrained and well-mannered as Mandela, whom no one ever heard swear, to have seen that letter, with that language, in the South African press. His shame at the depths of vulgarity to which his wife had descended left him with no option. Both as a personal matter and in terms of the political need to retain his cultivated image of dignity, he had to declare the marriage over.

In private, he had endured quite enough conjugal torture. I learned of one especially hurtful episode from a friend of Mandela some years later. Not long after the end of her trial, Winnie was due to fly to the United States on ANC-related business. She wanted to take Mpofu with her, and Mandela said she should not. Winnie agreed not to, but went with him anyway. Mandela phoned her at her hotel room in New York, and Mpofu answered the phone.

It was a dagger to the heart. His love for Winnie and his memories of her had sustained his morale, had revived his spirits when he flagged, during the grim prison years. His letters to her from Robben Island revealed a romantic, sensual side to his nature that no one but Winnie then knew. He wrote that his memories of her were as "summer rain" in the desert of his cell; he recalled "the electric current" that "flushed" through his blood as he looked at her photograph and imagined their caresses. And he made no secret of his need to believe in her. "Strength and supreme optimism runs through my blood because I know you love me," he wrote, while confessing in another letter how much he missed her and his children: "I have been fairly successful in putting on a mask behind which I have pined for the family, alone."

His letters, of which there were many more in this mood, showed that the longest of separations had failed to dim his passion. They also suggested the measure of the bitterness he must have felt as the truth dawned. Winnie's letter to her young lover had been the last straw—it had revealed to the world the miserable depth of his folly. The kernel of his private self that he most cherished had been sullied, transformed by Winnie into tawdry soap opera.

And yet, in the statement announcing the end of his marriage, Mandela said he parted from her with no recriminations, that his love for her remained undiminished. Could that be true? Or was it just an attempt to paper over his humiliation with some measure of self-respect?

On the face of it, he was a man more sinned against than sinner, but he did not see it that way. At least at that particular point in his life, he still remained willing to accept that there had been mitigating factors in Winnie's fall from grace—and those mitigating factors all pointed to him. He took partial responsibility for the choices Winnie made, and accepted his share of guilt. It was his belief that the original sin was to have put his political cause before his family.

Mandela's first marriage to Evelyn Mase, with whom he had four children, had suffered those consequences as well. The couple broke up in part because Mandela had had some affairs of his own in the fifties, but also because, as Mandela himself would explain it, she had issued him with an ultimatum: he had to choose between her and the ANC. I met Evelyn in 1989. A Jehovah's Witness, she was a small, gentle woman who ran a rural shop, and seemed relieved that her marriage to Mandela had ended when it did.

Winnie, whose personality could not have been more different from Evelyn's, accepted the complete Mandela package (freedom fighting and all) while little knowing what it contained. Her father, however, predicted at their wedding that the marriage would be, as he put it, "no bed of roses." It turned out to be a vale of tears. His wife and family suffered without him, as he would acknowledge when he finally left prison, and, far more, as he saw it, than he had behind bars. Mandela, powerless to help, experienced the anguish in jail of believing it was all his fault. Had he not opted for the role of commander in chief of the armed wing of the ANC, he could have been a father to his family at home. But he could not do both, and it had been reckless of him to think he might.

Mandela's children paid a high price, too. He would never cease to feel he had failed them, and for the rest of his days relations within the family would remain fraught. Even his grandchildren were not saved from the consequences of his decision to pour the lion's share of his time and energy into political life. I remember a story I heard not long after his release. Mandela was accompanying one of his grandsons, who was about twenty, to buy his first car. The two arrived at the dealer's together, but then a crowd gathered around Mandela and swallowed him up. The young man felt the grip of his grandfather's hand loosen before he disappeared altogether, leaving him alone and ignored as the faceless masses, to whom Mandela had dedicated his life, danced and sang his praise.

Despite everything, Mandela did believe when he left prison that he would find a way to reconcile political and family life. Some years after his separation from Winnie, I interviewed a close friend of his, Amina Cachalia, who had known him since before he met Winnie, in 1957. "His one great wish," she told me, "was that he would come out of prison, and have a family life again with his wife and the children. Because he's a great family man and I think he really wanted that more than anything else and he couldn't have it." The sad, cruel and perhaps inevitable irony of Mandela's life, his greatest personal tragedy, was that he never managed to satisfy his longings for a stable family life. He could not have it both ways. His decision to opt wholeheartedly for political struggle was the determining factor, but his fallout with Winnie only deepened the catastrophe, contaminating his relationships with other family members, among them his daughter Zindzi.

Zindzi was a far more complicated character than I had imagined when I chatted with her cheerfully in her mother's kitchen over fried eggs. At that very moment, in late January 1990, her current lover, the father of her third child, was in a prison cell. Five days later he hanged himself. Zindzi, as I came to understand, was very much her mother's daughter, inheriting her capacity to dissemble, as well as her strength of personality. She was also politically more engaged than the rest of Mandela's children.

In 1985, the then-president of South Africa, P. W. Botha, sought to silence the global clamor for Mandela's freedom by agreeing to release him if he unconditionally rejected violence as a political weapon. Winnie was still in forced exile then, far away in the Orange Free State, and it fell to Zindzi to deliver his response in a letter he wrote from prison that she read out before a packed political rally in a Soweto stadium. "I cherish my own freedom dearly, but I care even more for your freedom," the letter said. "Only free men can negotiate . . . I cannot and will not give any undertaking at a time when I and you, the people, are not free. Your freedom and mine cannot be separated."

It was a clear statement that he put the interests of his people above those of his and his family's welfare. Whether Zindzi grasped that at the time I do not know, but the unhappiness and sheer chaos that she would endure in her own private life, a mirror of her mother's, did find expression in a succession of tense episodes with her father after he was set free.

One of them took place before friends and family on the day of her marriage to the father of her fourth child, six months after her parent's separation. It was a glittering occasion at Johannesburg's swankiest hotel, with Zindzi radiant in a magnificent pearl and sequin bridal dress. It seemed to be a joyous celebration; in truth, it provided further evidence of the Mandela family's dysfunction.

One of the guests was a white politician called Helen Suzman, a good friend of Mandela's who was the same age as he was and had visited him several times in jail. At the wedding, Suzman sat near the top table, where Mandela, Winnie, and other family members sat with the bride and groom. Suzman told me that Mandela went through the ceremonial motions with all the propriety one would have expected. He joined in the cutting of the wedding cake and played his part when the time came to give his speech, declaring, "She's not mine now," as fathers are supposed to do in such circumstances. He did not, however, mention Winnie in the speech. When he sat down, he looked silent and cheerless.

Maybe he had had time to reflect in the intervening six months on the depth of Winnie's betrayal. For, indeed, more details soon emerged of her love affairs while her husband was in prison, and of the crimes of the gang of young men—"Winnie's boys," as they were known in Soweto—who played the role of both bodyguards and courtly retinue during the last four years of Mandela's incarceration. They had not just killed Stompie Moeketsi, the fourteen-year-old boy who she had been found guilty of assaulting and kidnapping; they had killed at least two more young black men, beat up Winnie's perceived enemies, and raped young girls, mostly with impunity. Whether Mandela chose to realize it at the time, he was the reason that she never ended up going to jail. Some years later, the minister of justice and the chief of national intelligence admitted to me that they had conveyed a message to the relevant members of the judiciary to show Winnie leniency. Mandela's mental and emotional well-being were essential to the success of the negotiations between the government and the ANC; for him to bow out of the process could have had catastrophic consequences for the country as a whole. Jailing Winnie would be too grave a risk.

It would have been hard enough as it was, even without

his old enemies' help, to preserve his equilibrium. Winnie had betrayed him as a man and, through her crimes, had traduced the values he strove to embody. By the time Zindzi's wedding had come around, the scales had well and truly lifted.

Bizarrely, and almost inexplicably, one of the guests at the wedding, prominently positioned near the top table, was the "white hag" Winnie had derided in her letter to Mpofu, the lover for whom he had left Winnie and with whom he had had a child. Sitting next to her was a man I knew to be a former lover of Winnie's from the eighties. I had spoken to him at length and he had told me so. It was hard to imagine that Mandela himself had not found out. It also would have been difficult for him to miss the menacing glances Winnie cast toward Dali's ex-lover, though hopefully he missed the moment during the wedding reception when Winnie brushed past her and hissed at him, signaling her with his head, "Go on! Take her! Take her!"

When the band struck up a waltz and the newly married couple got up to dance, Mandela, who had been standing up, turned his back on Winnie and returned stiffly to his place at the top table. Grim-faced for the rest of the night, he treated Winnie as if she didn't exist. At one point, Helen Suzman passed him a note. "Smile, Nelson," it said.

Whether it was true that he felt no recriminations toward Winnie at the time of his separation, he manifestly did now. Whether his love for her remained, even in some inscrutable corner of his heart, seemed unlikely. The shared responsibility he felt for her sins had been diminished by his growing awareness of the extent of her betrayal. He had also reflected, as he would reveal later in his divorce proceedings, that however many mitigating factors there may have been, other women in her position, whose husbands had faced long jail sentences, had not behaved the way in which she had. He thought in particular of his best friend's wife, Albertina Sisulu, a high-profile political activist who had also been persecuted by the security police, but who eased happily back into married life when her husband Walter returned home after twenty-five years in prison.

In October 1994, five months after Mandela had become president, I spoke to a friend of Mandela's, one of the very few people in whom he confided the details of his marital difficulties. The friend leaned over to me at one point in the conversation and said, "You know, it's amazing. He has forgiven all his political enemies, but he cannot forgive her."

A year and a half later, in March 1996, he made his feelings towards Winnie public at the Rand Supreme Court in Johannesburg, the very place where he had accompanied and supported Winnie during her trial in 1991. He pled for his divorce and won the case, yet, as his lawyer Wim Trengrove would tell me later, "He was arbitrarily generous about sharing his estate with her, giving her what was more than fair." But before making that concession, he made his feelings bluntly known in court. Standing a few feet away from Winnie, he addressed the judge, saying, "Can I put it simply, my lord? If the entire universe tried to persuade me to reconcile with the defendant, I would not. . . . I am determined to get rid of this marriage." He did not shirk from describing before the court the disappointment and misery of married life after he returned from prison. Winnie, he explained, did not share his bed once in the two years following their reunion. "I was the loneliest man," he said.

Anthony Sampson, his official biographer, remarked to me how sadly ironic it was that Mandela should simultaneously have been the most famous man in the world and the loneliest. A friend of Mandela's since before his imprisonment, Sampson wrote in his excellent biography, "[B]ehind all his gregariousness he still maintains an impenetrable reserve, defending his private hinterland." When I read those lines, I think again of Mandela as the chairman of a nineteenth century London gentlemen's club. Such individuals had immense social aplomb but were temperamentally aloof, emotionally walled up. They were driven by what the Victorian poet Arthur Hugh Clough called "terrible notions of duty" that boost the public figure but can stunt the private man. It is impossible to avoid concluding that he was far less at ease in private than in public life. In the harsh world of South African politics he had his bearings, in the family sphere he often seemed baffled and lost.

Happily for his country, one did not drain energy from the other. Thanks to a kind of self-imposed apartheid of the mind, personal anguish and the political drive inhabited separate compartments, and ran along parallel lines. He was able to govern his feelings. Winnie had indicated as much in the interview I did with her at her home just before his release. As out of control as she could be in her personal affairs, she possessed a lucid political intelligence, and a mature understanding of where her husband's priorities lay, even if she deluded herself in attributing some of his qualities to herself. "When you lead the kind of life we lead, if you are involved in a revolutionary situation, you cease to think in terms of self," she said. "The question of personal feelings and reactions does not even arise because you are in a position where you think solely in terms of the nation, the people who have come first all your life."

Precisely such a need to put his people before himself came to Mandela's rescue at the moment of his deepest personal despair. However unhappy he might have been, many of those to whom he had chosen to dedicate his life were enduring horrors far greater than any he had known. The process of political transition he endeavored to steer by peaceful means was under threat of collapse as those who feared democracy waged a war of terror on Soweto and other black townships on Johannesburg's periphery. Thousands were dying and, as Mandela warned at the time, if the violence did not abate, South Africa would drown in blood. The gravity of the situation provided him with the necessary perspective to put his personal troubles to one side. He was his people's anointed leader and to wallow in his own pain now, of all times, would be to succumb to the cardinal sin of self-indulgence. Family relationships belonged on a plane of unfathomable complexity where his sure-footed political judgment and clairvoyant leadership offered neither comfort nor light. The incentive was now greater than ever to perform in the terrain where he was strongest, get the politics right, and navigate his people to freedom.

4

# WOOING THE BLACKS

On the very evening that Mandela announced the end of his marriage, Blantina Radebe's seventeen-year-old son was killed—a black teenager shot in the back by black men urged by their black leader to fight in defense of apartheid. It was no isolated incident. The death of the boy was the consequence of a shadowy, murderous campaign to spark war in South Africa's black townships. In the half century that Mandela had dedicated to the liberation struggle, never had so much blood been shed as in the years immediately following his release from prison. His challenge was to stop a far worse escalation by preventing his people from rising to the bait, persuading them to do as he had done and curb the impulse for vengeance.

For Blantina Radebe, it was already too late. She was past the consolation that democracy or anything else could offer, as I found when I spoke to her at her home in the township of Katlehong, just east of Johannesburg, four days after her son's death. She had been unable to get out of bed since. She lay there propped up on her pillows fully dressed inside a darkened room as she told me what had happened. Her elderly mother sat at the foot of the bed, her head in her hands.

"He was very sweet, my boy. He was very soft," said Mrs. Radebe, speaking slowly, mournfully. "His name was Simon. He was seventeen and still at school." Mrs. Radebe received news in the middle of the night that Simon had been shot. "At five next morning, I went out on my own to the hostel where the Zulus of Inkatha live and I found his body lying outside on the ground. A man came out of the hostel. He looked at me—he looked happy—and he said: 'Why leave the children out here? We're going to come out and eat them.' Then I turned and saw there was another body lying nearby. It was Simon's friend Aubrey Mashego. Aubrey was also at school. He was eighteen."

The hostel, a feature of every township around Johannesburg, was a dingy, densely packed, forbidding fortress where only men lived, migrant workers from rural areas who had left their families to come to the African continent's richest metropolis for work. The majority of the hostel inhabitants were illiterate, traditionally tribal, politically malleable Zulus, the constituency from which the right wing organization Inkatha, implacably hostile to the ANC, and its all-powerful chief, Mangosuthu Buthelezi, drew its support. Lacking the numbers to compete with the ANC in a national election, Buthelezi feared he had more to lose than to win from black people getting the vote. So, decidedly, did far right groups within the white state, appalled by President de Klerk's decision to release Mandela and negotiate the terms of a new system of rule with the ANC. Drawn together by their common fears, Inkatha and recalcitrant elements within the police and military formed a secret alliance of terror. The job of the Inkatha warriors was to do the dirty work.

It was wrenching to witness Blantina Radebe's grief and,

while speaking to freshly bereaved mothers became almost routine for me during my time in South Africa, it still moves me as I recall the scene today, two decades later. "He was on a train on the way to visit his uncle with Aubrey and two other friends," she said. "Some men with guns came up to them, asked them their names and then said: 'Sit down, Mandela's children. Sit down, Radebe. Today is your last day.' " How did she know this? "The two boys who survived told me. They live across the road."

Blantina began to weep. Her mother stood up and hugged her. I went across the road and found the two boys. Llewellyn Motloung and Soli Ngubeni, both eighteen, had been shot but managed to escape. Llewellyn had bandages over his shoulder and a heavily swollen chin. A bullet fired from close range had penetrated Soli's right buttock, just missing his hip bone.

"There were about fifty of them inside the train carriage, six of them had guns and others knives," Llewellyn said. "One tall, tough man dressed completely in black asked us if we were ANC. We said no. Then he said: 'You're not telling the truth. You're on your way to the hostel to hit us. You'll see. When we get to the hostel our boys there will kill you.' "

The four boys were forced off the train at the next station where a dozen men grabbed them and took them across the road into the hostel. "They took us to a campus inside, in the middle, and then asked us questions about the ANC and Mandela," Llewellyn said, noting that all the Inkatha men were wearing red bandannas. I asked the boys if they were ANC members. Soli, who happened to be the one Zulu among the four, shook his head. "We don't belong to any political organization." So, why did the Inkatha men think they were with the ANC? "Because they said we were born in the township and all people born in the township were ANC."

The four boys—Soli, Llewellyn, Aubrey, and Simon—were

kept under guard in the hostel all afternoon. It was not hard for me to imagine the terror they must have felt. On another occasion, in the same neighborhood, I remembered seeing a different set of teenage boys in the back of an armored police vehicle surrounded by two dozen shouting Inkatha men with machetes, spears, and knobkerries—ceremonial Zulu clubs deployed in those days as weapons for killing people suspected of belonging to the ANC. The Inkatha men were in a celebratory mood, hurling insults at the boys, gloatingly letting them know they would soon get their hands on them. I implored the white police officer in charge not to hand them over to the Inkatha men. He said he would not but, just in case, when he wasn't looking I put my head into the cramped, dark armored vehicle to try and get the four young men's names and addresses. I planned to check later if the policeman had stuck by his word. But I couldn't get anything out of them. Their teeth were chattering so hard that they could not talk. I have always wondered what became of them.

Soli and Llelwellyn barely survived their own horror movie. When darkness fell, said Soli, a man appeared on a bicycle at the hostel with a large blue bag draped over the handlebars. "About ten guys formed a queue and each of them took a gun from inside the bag. Then they pushed us outside the hostel, on to the tar road, and lined us up as if we were going to start a race. Then they said 'run.' We ran and they started firing."

Simon and Aubrey were killed. Llewellyn, shot in the shoulder, found refuge in a house half a mile away. Soli, bleeding from a bullet in his buttock, ran five miles to his home. They had not been ANC before the attack, they said, but they would be now. Inkatha was the enemy. They would avenge their friends. "I will await my chance," said Soli, "and I will kill those people."

I never saw Soli or Llewellyn again. I never knew whether they killed, or were killed or whether, for all the bluster of the moment, they fled their homes in search of a quieter life.

Their story, sad and harrowing as it was, was entirely typical in those days. To hear such accounts in the townships around Johannesburg—in Katlehong, Soweto, Thokoza, Vosloorus, Alexandra, Tembisa, Sebokeng—became almost routine to me. The pattern was always the same. Inkatha people living in the hostels attacked young men who lived in neighboring homes and whom they assumed, in almost all cases correctly, to be sympathetic to the ANC; the young men who survived vowed to organize themselves and fight back.

Mandela sought to persuade them, despite enormous provocation, not to do so. The Inkatha killings were the latest and most savage of the crimes his people had endured under apartheid. His Herculean task was to reroute the river of black anger and frustration away from revenge and toward the green pastures of reconciliation.

This was not, in the first place, a moral question for Mandela; it was not a matter of turning the other cheek because it was the heavenly ordained thing to do. Straight, cold, practical politics governed Mandela's thinking. Should a logic of bloody reprisals set in, the eventual outcome could only be civil war, with all sectors of the population obliged to take sides. War was democracy's enemy; war was not the terrain where the ANC, or black people in general, were strongest. The ANC's strength rested on its numbers and its talents, particularly Mandela's, in negotiation.

Continued bloodletting dragged the center of South African politics away from the negotiating table and toward pitched battles in the townships. Images still linger in my mind of walls of young black bodies piled up in police yards; of bodies in the back of a police van with blood gushing out from between legs, where genitals had been cut; of an Inkatha massacre of forty-seven innocents, among them a nine-month-old baby wrapped in a white sheet; of whooping Zulu warriors, back in their hostel after a foray, holding up their victims' dismembered hands as trophies of war. These scenes of savagery took place a mere ten or twenty miles away from the modern conference building next to the Johannesburg airport where the negotiating teams of the ANC, the government, and other interested parties met day after day in smoke-filled rooms. But in spirit and in atmosphere they were worlds away.

The ANC had very able people sitting in those rooms, more than capable of outwitting government negotiators in a high-stakes poker game played out over a period of three years. Mandela only rarely made an appearance, preferring to play a strategic role behind the scenes. The tougher challenge was stopping township violence, which he soon understood to be the sharp end of a conspiracy designed to render the negotiations meaningless. If his people were sucked into a vengeful spiral of war, the high-level talks would remain just that—high-level talks of no relevance to the realities on the ground.

Years later, the South African political transition would come to be regarded as exemplary by international experts involved in conflict resolution, a burgeoning profession amidst the global disorder that followed the end of the Cold War. When people use the word "revolution" in the South African context, they usually place the adjective "peaceful" in front of it. South Africa did move from tyranny to democracy after a process of talks generally held in a civilized spirit of give and take. The problem with taking a one-dimensionally rosy perspective on "the South African miracle" is the fact that, parallel to the talks, South Africa experienced its bloodiest bout of killings since the end of the Anglo-Boer War nearly a century earlier. More than ten thousand people died in political violence in the Johannesburg area alone during the four and a half years following Mandela's release. Many Blantina Radebes paid a dreadfully high price for their freedom.

The two phenomena, the talks and the killings, were not entirely unconnected. If Mandela had not been released, preparing the way for negotiations and apartheid's overthrow, the violence too would not have been unleashed. This is an extraordinarily obvious thing to say in retrospect, but at the time there were numerous commentators, almost all of them white and pontificating from the safe comfort of their homes or universities, who insisted on viewing the killings as a spontaneous black-on-black occurrence, a symptom of barbarous tribal enmity. "We understand our blacks," they would tell me. They did not. The truth was complicated. In essence, what we witnessed were the last dying kicks of the apartheid beast.

Mandela repeatedly denounced the existence of a hidden hand behind the violence. He described it as a "Third Force," a clandestine group within the security forces operating invisibly but actively to stoke war between Inkatha and the ANC. These far right sympathizers formed an alliance with Buthelezi that seemed unlikely at first, until one reflected that both had prospered from apartheid.

The racist system's most ambitious goal had always been to make the separation between blacks and whites more complete by creating a patchwork of blacks-only rural homelands, or *bantustans*, within South Africa's borders which would be self-ruled along tribal lines. Buthelezi played along with this game, accepting the Kwa-Zulu homeland (and the state money that came with it) as his personal fiefdom. He presided as chief minister over a little sham of a parliament inside which Inkatha exercised one-party rule. The governments of both Margaret Thatcher and Ronald Reagan went along with the farce during the 1980s, lured by the pro-free-market noises and anti-apartheid pieties that Buthelezi would parrot to the press. He acted the part of aspiring democrat, hoping they'd believe that he represented South Africa's best hope for the future, a better choice of black leadership than the still imprisoned Mandela, whom some Western powers regarded as a Communist and a terrorist.

Inkatha had already been waging war for five years on behalf of the apartheid state against the 50 percent of the Zulu population in their territory who supported the goals of the ANC. The security police and military intelligence of the South African ruling party supplied the brains, the guns, and the organization, and Inkatha's Zulu battalions—always decked out in red bandanas so that they would not mistakenly kill their own—supplied the murderous brawn. Those loyal to the ANC had to choose between lying low and waiting to be massacred, or fighting back—they chose the latter, and the so-called black-on-black violence was born. After Mandela came out of prison, the bloody conspiracy was exported wholesale from Kwa-Zulu to the Johannesburg area, Mandela's home and South Africa's political heartland. Inkatha agitators under orders from faceless white men in the security services manipulated their troops into believing that if they did not kill first, they themselves would be victims. The regular, uniformed police on the ground often formed armed shields to protect Inkatha hostels from counterattacks by township residents while doing nothing to investigate the killings and massacres.

Buthelezi was regarded by the majority of black South Africans as apartheid's monstrous puppet. But he did not lack the ability to think for himself. As a foreign ambassador in Pretoria put it to me once, Buthelezi was "mad as a fox." There was method in his paranoia. He was deft at playing conservatives abroad and his white admirers at home, telling them what they wanted to hear, convincing them that he, not Mandela, was the black leader they should trust. I remember a speech at a rally in the township of Thokoza, in which he invoked God's name ten times. When he spoke in Zulu, he stoked tribal antagonism, conjuring dread, urging upon his spear-wielding followers the need to stand up in defense of the menaced Zulu nation. When he spoke in English, he portrayed himself as a pious Christian leader (he was in the habit then of inviting his white supporters to prayer breakfasts) calling on black brother to stop killing black brother, indignantly denying any role in the killings. Even as 3,000 men in red headbands and spears stood before him agitating for war, he declared: "All the reports that one hears about people with red bands being Inkatha people is just so much political hogwash."

At the end of that speech in Thokoza, Buthelezi's Zulu battalions marched triumphantly through the townships, a moving forest of spears, firing shots in the air. The police looked on. Since his white admirers would not dream of going anywhere near a place like Thokoza, there was no chance of seeing with their own eyes what was going on. Buthelezi, a Dickensian caricature of unctuous hypocrisy, was able to say what they wanted to hear and they, watching on SABC TV, cheerfully took him at his word.

His tribal followers received an entirely different message. One winter's morning in Vooslorus, at the end of a typical morning's slaughter, I ventured up to the hostel across the road from the local police station, behind whose walls the Inkatha warriors had retreated. I felt safe because Buthelezi's followers had been taught to remain as much in awe of white people as in colonial times. Besides, it was a golden rule of the Inkatha not to harm white people, for fear of upsetting his carefully crafted message of Christian brotherliness.

I entered the hostel and walked into a large central yard,

like the one Simon Radebe and his three friends had been held in. I was met by twenty young men carrying spears who led me to a gray-bearded elder who, they said, would answer my questions. The elder, though he would not tell me his name, had a straightforward explanation for why they were going on the rampage, terrorizing the neighborhood residents. "The problem is Mandela," he said, "because he is taken to be the king now and Chief Buthelezi is not seen as the king anymore." So, Buthelezi had to become the king again? "Exactly." And how would they do that? "Fighting against those who say Mandela is king."

The message conveyed was brutally simple. Letting the will of the people take its course would cause Mandela, not Buthelezi, to be South Africa's leader; the solution was to kill those people, because anything further removed from Mandela's notion of how politics should be conducted was hard to imagine. Behind the barbarity of the chiefs was an orchestrated offensive against Mandela's democratic project, guided by Inkatha's friends, advisers, and arms suppliers within the apartheid security machine. This much would be revealed and anatomized in detail both by a judicial commission of inquiry and, after Mandela came to power, by a Truth and Reconciliation Commission.

None of it would have been possible without the engine of Buthelezi's emotional volatility. Buthelezi's rage and envy at the arrival of the real king on a stage he had previously dominated was compounded by what I always interpreted to be his terror that on the day democracy arrived he would be strung up by Mandela's triumphant followers. President de Klerk and his ministers never believed such a fate would await them, but Buthelezi, I believe, did. His historical precedents came from the royal Zulu bloodline to which he belonged. In the 19th

century Zulu kings replaced Zulu kings in an often repeated
pattern of betrayal and bloody revenge.

Mandela, who had a number of bizarre private encounters
with Buthelezi, seemed to believe he was mentally unstable. He
indicated as much to me in a hotel in central Johannesburg,
at the end of one of the many press conferences of his I attended. I went up to the podium after the event was over for a
chat and he turned and said to me, "Chief Buthelezi, you know
he is a bit . . ." He left the sentence hanging but completed his
point by tapping his right index finger on the side of his fore-
head. I cannot remember what I said in response but I guess it
must have been something along the lines of, "I couldn't agree
more." It would have made for a dynamite news story, but I
didn't report it. That had been a private exchange between
Mandela and myself and, besides, if I had made it public, God
alone knew how many more Simon Radebes might have died
in retaliation.

Mandela, who went out to the embattled townships more
than any other senior ANC leader, was at least as angry with
de Klerk as he was with Buthelezi, whom he had the wisdom
to treat in private with the ego-massaging deference best employed with the dangerously insecure. The South African president did not have emotional instability as an excuse. Mandela
had described him as "a man of integrity" on emerging from
prison as a gesture of goodwill designed to launch negotiations in an atmosphere of mutual trust. Mandela did not believe de Klerk was actively complicit in the Inkatha conspiracy,
but he became convinced that he was doing nothing to stop it.
De Klerk's inaction in the face of the slaughter of thousands
of black people ensured that Mandela never called him a man
of integrity again. Mandela's discovery that de Klerk, for all
his fine reformist language, was at heart another conservative-

minded Afrikaner who placed far more value on white lives than on black ones made for soured relations. Mandela said it to his face in private meetings and he said it in public: had it been white people dying like flies the president would have deployed the security forces with unstoppable force.

Mandela revealed his feelings at a long meeting with senior Afrikaner journalists. He wanted them on his side, but a line had been crossed and this time he gave them a stern lecture. The message he endeavored to deliver was simple, but necessary: blacks were human beings just as much as they were. He asked if their reaction to the ANC's movement might be more empathetic if it had been whites who were dying violent deaths in the suburbs every day. He reminded the journalists of a recent case when a white farmer had been murdered and the police had mounted a vast hunt, complete with helicopters, for the killers. But for all the killings of black men and women in the townships, there had been next to no investigations, let alone arrests.

Mandela had not factored the mass slaughter of his people into his calculations when he mapped out the journey from apartheid to democracy in his prison cell. He never imagined that he and the ANC would find themselves issuing calls to the United Nations and the European Community to send in peace monitors to do the work that the police should have been doing. De Klerk, in his blinkered ignorance, failed to see causes of the violence, but his inaction was all the more curious because he understood its dimension and the threat it contained. Twice, he warned publicly of civil war.

Under the relentless weight of evidence presented by Mandela in their private meetings, finally de Klerk did act. He was left with no choice but to recognize that members of his security forces had engaged in violent and dirty tricks to obstruct political change. In December 1992, he fired six generals and suspended or retired twenty-three officers, but for some of the embattled townships around Johannesburg, the president's intervention came too late. After two and a half years, the violence had already acquired a momentum of its own.

Mandela still had a huge problem on his hands. He understood all too well the growing fervor among his own supporters for the ANC to respond in kind. He himself, after all, had been the original commander of the ANC's armed wing, the prime mover behind the organization's 1960 decision to resort to violence against the state. He understood even better that the government was more ripe for a political deal with the black majority than it had ever been, and that to go to war against Inkatha and their backers in the security forces would be to play into their hands. Drowning the country in blood was their goal, not his. Instead, he had to take the long view and try to turn his people away from the short-term satisfactions of violent retribution.

This test was difficult enough when anonymous young men were dying daily in the townships; it became close to insuperable when the forces of the far right that shared Buthelezi's fears killed any man they considered a threat. Chris Hani, the second most popular leader in the ANC after Mandela, was assassinated on the morning of April 10, 1993, outside his home in Boksburg, a previously whites-only suburb two miles down the road from Katlehong. The negotiations had been stumbling on despite continuing township violence, but suddenly they felt like an irrelevant sideshow. The fear now wasn't that the democratic project would go up in flames, but that the whole country would. How far could one push the patience of black South Africans? And, for that matter, of Mandela?

Hani had been the last leader of the ANC's armed wing, the most charismatic of Mandela's successors in that role. It was true that the armed struggle was largely a myth, but it was a powerful myth, especially among the black youth in whom the ANC's political energy was most convincingly concentrated.

When Mandela and Hani met, after emerging respectively from prison and from exile, they discovered they were kindred spirits. Hani had the same natural antipathy to using violence for political ends, but, like Mandela, he believed that his enemies had left him with no choice. Hani became like a son to Mandela—the politically engaged son he never had. Mandela's sense of personal loss was sharp, but, once again, he knew he had to subdue his own private feelings for the public good. Immediately upon hearing the news of Hani's death, he weighed the political consequences and judged that the project of political transformation for which he had sacrificed his personal happiness had never been under more immediate threat.

Members of the press had spent the previous three years swinging between the perception that the process of change was on track, to the fear that it would be fatally derailed. But now we felt there was no going back. "Staring Into The Abyss," screamed the headlines in South African newspapers. And they did not seem to be exaggerating. Surely black South Africans, many of whom had only grudgingly gone along with Mandela's message of forgiveness and reconciliation, would finally give way to the impulse for vengeance. All the more so when it emerged within hours of Hani's assassination that the suspected killer was a white man. I heard the news of his arrest on the car radio on the way to Thokoza, a township that had endured as much violence over the previous three years as Katlehong. On arrival, I found the mood as dark as I had expected. One young man I talked to was called, of all things, Macbeth.

This was too much, Macbeth said. "There's a lot of pain. Not just because of Comrade Chris—many others have been killed before him. We should have taken action before. Now we should take revenge. Now we should take up arms against the enemy." Macbeth captured the mood of every young man I spoke to in Thokoza.

On the drive out of the township I put on the radio again and heard more chilling news. An angry crowd had burned two white men to death and cut out the tongue of a third near Cape Town, a part of South Africa that had not endured anything like the same degree of violence as the Johannesburg area. An ANC spokesman in Cape Town warned that South Africa was "going to pay a very big price for the loss of Chris Hani."

Other ANC leaders strove to appeal for calm but the tension remained high. Mandela was the one person in South Africa with any hope of tempering the public mood. Three days after Hani's killing, Mandela went, with de Klerk's blessing, on national radio and television. He had just one thing going for him: the killer, an expatriate Pole, and an accomplice from the far right Conservative Party, with whom Inkatha would soon forge a formal alliance, had been arrested. He had been caught because a white woman, an Afrikaner neighbor of Hani's, had the presence of mind to jot down the license number of the getaway car. Mandela turned the bravery of the woman, who had to go into hiding for fear of reprisals from the far right, to his advantage, reminding his angry followers, right at the start of his address, that it was thanks to a white compatriot that the culprits had been caught.

"Tonight I am reaching out to every single South African, black and white, from the very depths of my being," he said. "A white man, full of prejudice and hate, came to our country and committed a deed so foul that our whole nation now teeters on the brink of disaster. A white woman, of Afrikaner origin, risked her life so that we may know and bring to justice this assassin."

Mandela's uncharacteristic use of a phrase as emotionally charged as "from the depths of my being," revealed the extent of his alarm and his awareness that he had to call on every last grain of authority gleaned from his twenty-seven years in prison to make his appeal stick. Formally, he was addressing himself to black and white South Africans, but no one was in any doubt that his own people were the true intended audience. The message he sought to convey was clear: not all white people should be tarred with the same brush as Hani's killers. Indiscriminate violence against whites would not only be a violation of the core principle he and his organization stood for, it would also be deeply unjust. It was the courageous woman, not the hateful man, who should be held up as the genuine representative of white South Africa.

In order for Mandela's deeper call for restraint to take root, he had to first identify with his people's pain, then challenge his followers to control their vengeful impulses, just as he had. He described Hani's death as a national tragedy that had rightly caused grief and anger, but that grief and anger threatened to tear the country apart. "We must not permit ourselves to be provoked by people who seek to deny us the very freedom for which Chris Hani gave his life." Any acts of violence now would mean trampling on the values that Chris Hani stood for.

"Those who commit such acts serve only the interests of the assassins and desecrate his memory . . . With all the authority at my command, I appeal to all our people to remain calm and to honor the memory of Chris Hani by remaining a disciplined force for peace."

Never had the urgency been greater, and never had he invoked all the authority at his command. This was an order from the unofficial commander in chief, and to disobey it would be treason to the cause.

Mandela's appeal had its intended effect. South Africa stepped back from the abyss, black people did as Mandela bade them, and white people heaved a collective sigh of relief. It was because of Mandela's reaction at that moment, more than any other, that Archbishop Tutu, the most lucid commentator on the South African political scene, believed that Mandela had been the key to South Africa's peaceful transition to democracy. "If he hadn't been around, the country would, in fact, have torn itself apart," Tutu would tell me years later. "Had Mandela not gone on television and radio . . . our country would have gone up in flames. It would have been the easiest thing just to release the dogs of war. That is what maybe many of the younger Turks had wanted to see happen. Mercifully, he was there and held them all at bay."

I watched Mandela hold a particularly angry set of young men at bay three and a half months after Hani's death. The stakes were not as high, but Mandela's performance was at least as impressive. Katlehong and neighboring townships adjoined the area where Chris Hani had lived, where the cumulative rage was greatest and the ANC's young Macbeths bayed most for blood. This was the last redoubt of the township violence and it had acquired its own unstoppable tit-for-tat dynamic. ANC youths had organized themselves into what they called "self-defense units," but after Hani's death they had gone on the offensive against Inkatha hostel dwellers, who then launched counterattacks of their own.

On a Tuesday morning in the first week of July 1993, I went to the hospital that served Katlehong, and found a young man in blue-and-white-striped pajamas who sat upright in his bed blowing bubbles—not through his mouth but through his neck. He lay among thirty-four other patients, all of them shot or stabbed, all of them fortunate to have survived the worst night of political violence any South African township had seen that year. Between sunset and sunrise, forty-five people were killed in Katlehong. In the previous thirty-six hours, another twenty-four had died here and in neighboring Thokoza.

The young man in the blue and white pajamas had a three-inch tube sticking out of his throat, just above his Adam's apple. The hole into which the tube had been fitted was made by a bullet. He was breathing through the tube. Or gurgling, rather. Hence the bubbles—light pink, blood bubbles. Next to him was Linda Shweni, who had been shot in the thigh, the face, and the nape of the neck. He was in pain but able to talk. He said he was seventeen and attended school. His story echoed that of Blantina Radebe's son and his three friends fifteen months earlier. Little had changed since then for the people here.

Linda said he had been driving near Katlehong's male hostel, the one where Simon Radebe and his friends had been held captive, when a group of men opened fire on them. "Three of us were lucky," Linda said. "We were wounded and brought to hospital. I don't know what happened to our other friend. He was wounded but he has disappeared, like the car. Maybe they took him into the hostel. They often do that, then they kill the people."

Violence continued to escalate over the next weeks. Mandela's appeal for discipline and calm had reached the rest of the country, but it had fallen on deaf ears here. After 130 people died on the last weekend of July 1993, he judged the time had come to deliver his message in person.

The date was August 5, 1993. The venue, a dusty local soccer stadium. The security measures were enormous. By venturing into that most volatile of areas, Mandela was going into the lion's den and President de Klerk knew that it was in his interests as much as the ANC's to ensure that he wasn't harmed. Hani's death had provided a frightening glimpse of what would happen to South Africa in the event that Mandela suffered the same fate. It was a plausible scenario from the day of his release, but more so now in Katlehong where Inkatha gunmen, many with a limited understanding of the political repercussions of their actions, were on the loose.

To the alarm of Mandela's bodyguards, two of whom I'd get to know later, he had a reckless tendency to plunge into crowds. One told me how on a visit to New York, Mandela's convoy was stuck in traffic and he was going to be late for an appointment. So, ignoring his minders' calls, he stepped out of the car and strode down Sixth Avenue, to the amazement and wonder of passers by. Manhattan might have its perils, but it was not Katlehong and, while Mandela did seem to believe—with some justice—that he led a charmed life, this time he showed more restraint. With army helicopters circling noisily overhead and dozens of police and military vehicles on the ground, his car drove into the stadium and stopped in the middle of the field, where a table with a microphone marked the spot from which he would address his 10,000 followers.

I arrived an hour or so before he did, time enough to notice that a message had been scribbled on the table for him to see, a message that the local leaders organizing the event did not see fit to erase. It read, "No peace. Do not talk about peace. We've had enough. Please, Mr. Mandela, no peace. Give us weapons. No peace."

Mandela arrived to great singing and dancing, cries of "Long live the ANC!" and a call and response chant of "Amandla!" and "Ngawethu!" meaning "power," and "to the people." ANC rallies always followed a set liturgy, completed by the singing of the black anthem of resistance, "Nkosi Sikelel' iAfrika": God Bless Africa. Mandela's arrival in any black residential area unfailingly provoked delirium, but the mood was different today, and when Mandela read the note scribbled on the table, he was left in no doubt as to what that mood was. I saw him acknowledge the note's contents with a brief nod.

This time he spoke off the cuff. The days were long gone when the ANC felt it had to rein him in by making him read from a prepared text. Mandela had consolidated his leadership. Within the ANC's National Executive Committee, where policy was decided, he listened and sometimes even allowed his arguments to be overturned, but it was he who had the last word. Outside, addressing the public, he was the ANC's Moses, the voice who issued the commandments.

I stood behind him and a little to one side as he stepped up to the microphone, attentive to the crowd's reaction. His first task was to get the crowd on his side by making them understand, as he had done in his address after Hani's death, that he shared their anger. "The first big problem," he declared, "is the unwillingness of the government, the police, and the South African Defence Force to protect our people . . . to them the lives of black people are cheap. It is as if flies had died."

However, as the crowd quickly grasped, he had come not to praise ANC supporters in Katlehong, but to scold them. "There are times now," he said, "when our people participate in the killing of innocent people. It is difficult for us to say when people are angry that they must be nonviolent. . . . But the solution is peace, it is reconciliation, it is political tolerance."

The crowd shuffled uneasily, all the more so when he proposed that they should recognize that not all hostel dwellers were criminals. They should be allowed out of the hostel to go to the shops, to visit relatives freely, he said. The response was dismay. A murmur rose up. You could see people muttering to each other. Some jeered.

"No!" Mandela cried. "We must accept blacks are fighting each other in our townships. The task of the ANC is to unite black people as well as whites. . . . But the National Party of de Klerk, the police, the army are also involved and that makes the task more difficult." Back on familiar ground, the crowd warmed to him again.

The speech went back and forth like this for almost an hour, as if Mandela were engaging in a public dialogue with his supporters. Winning them over, receiving their applause, shocking them, responding to their shock, holding his ground. His boldest message came at the end.

"We must accept that responsibility for ending violence is not just the government's, the police's, the army's," he declared. "It is also our responsibility. . . . We should put our own house in order. If you have no discipline you are not freedom fighters. If you are going to kill innocent people you don't belong to the ANC."

You could sense that some of the crowd felt chastened, but many were simply flabbergasted. Did Mandela not know who had started the killings? Did he forget that the great majority of the victims had been his own supporters? He knew perfectly well, and said as much, but his underlying point held. At stake now was democracy in South Africa and it fell to the people to be disciplined soldiers, loyal to the greater good.

"Your task is reconciliation," he admonished them. "You must go to your area and ask a member of Inkatha: why are we fighting?" The crowd turned again. A loud murmur went up. They did not want to hear this.

"Listen to me! Listen to me!" he cried above the din. "I am your leader. As long as I am your leader I am going to give leadership. Do you want me to remain your leader?" Chastened, alarmed, confused they pondered the question. Mandela had issued them a challenge. "I ask you again, do you want me to remain your leader?" The crowd thought some more. This was Nelson Mandela, their hero, their leader, the father who had sacrificed all for them.

"Yeesss!" they bellowed back. "Yeeeeesss!" Mandela responded with a ghost of a smile and a curt nod of the head. Then, with a sharp, "I thank you," he declared the proceedings over.

Mandela had defeated the crowd and the crowd acknowledged his victory. With more relief than jubilation, grateful to have survived the close call, they rose to their feet, clapped their hands, swayed and, at the top of their voices, sang, "Nelson Mande-ehla! Nelson Mande-ehla!"

In the following weeks, the violence in Katlehong and neighboring townships eased. His speech had had its effect, but so also had the dawning reality that power was ebbing slowly from de Klerk to Mandela. The ANC and the National Party government were effectively partners now, with a common objective, and the police began to be more in line with the novel idea that, yes indeed, in the new South Africa, black lives had value, too.

The road was clear at last for the negotiations to reach their destination. Three months after Mandela's speech at Katlehong, on the night of November 17, 1993, he joined President de Klerk and nineteen other South African leaders at a ceremony to ratify the country's first democratic constitution. Breaking with forty-five years of apartheid, and three and a half centuries of white rule, the constitution's founding principle was that all people, black and white, stood equal before the law. A compromise agreement on a parallel electoral bill stipulated that the first post-apartheid government would be a coalition in which cabinet posts would be allocated in proportion to the total number of votes each party won, and April 27 was set for the country's first ever general elections.

"We are at the end of an era. We are at the beginning of a new era," Mandela declared. "Together we can build a society free of violence. We can build a society grounded on friendship and our common humanity—a society founded on tolerance. . . . Let us join hands and march into the future."

Not everyone shared the rosy vision of a democratic future. Buthelezi, who had not signed his name to the document, and whose Inkatha party had pulled out of the constitutional negotiations four months earlier, remained offstage, snarling. So did a new body led by a group of retired military generals calling itself the Afrikaner Volksfront. No friends of democracy, they threatened to go to war unless they were granted a separate Afrikaner state within South Africa's boundaries. Buthelezi, revealing his true colors for all to see, had gone into a political partnership with the Volksfront, joining forces under the banner of a remarkable new black and white movement dedicated to the perpetuation of apartheid that they chose to call the "Freedom Alliance."

# 5

# THE BITTER-ENDERS

**M**andela had one more dragon left to subdue, potentially the most fearsome of them all. He had forestalled a township war, he had conquered his own tortured heart, and he was beating down the apartheid state in negotiations, where his able lieutenants forced compromises from the de Klerk government they had never expected to make. But now, looming before him, glared the core of the Afrikaner far right, "the bitter-enders," as they were known in South Africa, heavily armed and bristling for war.

Mandela knew that, sooner or later, this was the final enemy he would have to confront and defeat if he was to fulfill his life's quest. He told me so in an interview I did with him at the end of April 1993, two weeks after Chris Hani's assassination. "Elements in the security forces, active and retired, covert organizations working underground" were prepared to go to any lengths to preserve the old order. "They want to plunge this country into a racist, bloody civil war," he said. "That is what they want and our task is to prevent that and ensure that elections, democratic elections, take place and a government of national unity is set up."

On May 6, 1993, the beast reared its head. That chilly night, in the town of Potchefstroom, seventy-five miles south-west of Johannesburg, disparate forces of the South African far right emerged from their caverns, resolved to make common cause against Mandela. They had turned a deaf ear to his message, and persisted in viewing Mandela as they had on the day of his release: as a Communist and a terrorist who should have been hanged. He had eased the worst fears of the white majority, but here in Potchefstroom, the founding home of the most racially exclusive branch of Afrikaner Christianity, his calls for peace went unheeded.

Fifteen thousand men, whose very identities were founded on the premise that whites were genetically superior to blacks, marched up and down the town, heavily armed, in brown shirts flaunting imitation Swastikas, pausing finally, at the ceremony's culmination, to listen to the barking oratory of their best-known leader, the white-bearded Eugene Terreblanche of the AWB, the Afrikaner Resistance Movement.

A keen student of Hitler's oratorical style, Terreblanche was a dangerous buffoon, whose followers had all served in the military, and many of whom had fought during the early eighties in South Africa's war against Communism in neighboring Angola. Presenting arms alongside the AWB was an outfit calling itself the Boer Resistance Movement, or Boere Weerstandsbeweging. The Boer Republican Army, Resistance Against Communism, the Afrikaner Monarchist Movement, the Foundation for Survival and Freedom, White Security, the White Resistance Movement, the Order of the Boer People, the Victory Commando, the White Wolves, and even the South African branch of the Ku Klux Klan were there. Many of them might have been dismissed as crazies in costumes, but all the movement needed was for fifty or one hundred men to take on their leaders' calls, and a campaign of terrorist bombings and assassinations could begin. Mandela feared that South Africa's fragile democratic scaffolding might come loose and that the country would be rent asunder.

Crude and simpleminded as they might have been, the leaders of the factions gathered at Potchefstroom had the basic political intelligence to understand that they would be more successful if united beneath one flag. The blacks had their leader; they needed one, too. They needed a champion who inspired respect and admiration, and had the courage and military know-how to lead them to final victory. Such a champion was in the crowd among them, awaiting the call.

His name was Constand Viljoen, a figure with a status almost as legendary among this fervid throng as Mandela's among black South Africans. Viljoen had been away in an exile of his own, on his family farm, but no white South African soldier had a more glorious reputation. A decorated veteran of the Angolan war, he had been the top commander of the South African Defense Force—army, air force, and navy—between 1980 and 1985. They were five of the most violent years of confrontation between black activists and the state, a period when military intelligence officers created political assassination squads, when wars were covertly fomented in neighboring countries, when troops quashed unrest in the black townships, and it became evident that white domination rested on the power of the gun. It was the general and his soldiers, not the civilians in government, who were apartheid's ultimate enforcers. Now General Viljoen was called upon to be apartheid's last line of defense.

At the climax of the Potchefstroom pageant, General Viljoen rose, to tumultuous applause, to the podium. Terreblanche announced that he would be "proud, proud" to serve as "a corporal" under the orders of this mightiest of living Afrikaner heroes and Viljoen, silver haired and martially up-right, solemnly accepted his anointment as commander in chief of a newly unified movement henceforth to be known as the Afrikaner Volksfront. Each of the organizations pres-ent took turns to come on stage and swear fealty to the man destiny had chosen to be the volk's savior in what they chose to see as their darkest hour. Then, entering into the spirit of the occasion, the general spoke, thundering against the "unholy alliance" between Mandela and de Klerk, declaring himself ready and willing to die in defense of the fatherland.

"You must pray for forgiveness for your sins," said Viljoen to his people, who believed as they always had that they were doing God's work, "and you must defend yourselves, for no one else will. Every Afrikaner must be ready. Every farm, every school is a target. If they attack our churches nowhere is safe. If we are stripped of our defensive capacity, we will be destroyed. A bloody conflict which will require sacrifices is inevitable, but we will gladly sacrifice because our cause is just."

The crowd was in ecstasy. "You lead, we will follow! You lead, we will follow!" they chanted. Vilojoen swore that he would lead them, and not just in defense of their culture, reli-gion, language, families, and homes, but also to the promised land, to apartheid's ultimate dream of a separate state within South Africa's existing borders, a territory of pure racial white-ness that he described, to a thunderous roar, as "an Israel for the Afrikaner." Their people had fought valiantly against the forces of British imperialism in the Anglo-Boer War of the late nineteenth and early twentieth century, Vilojoen reminded them. They would have to fight no less valiantly now. For, he declared, "the second Boer freedom struggle" had begun.

Mandela looked on in alarm. Word had reached him from intelligence sources that the general and a small group of retired senior military officers were able to assemble a force of one hundred thousand armed men. That might have been an exaggeration, but what Mandela did verify over the next three months was that Viljoen and his confidants had been traveling around the country, setting up clandestine cells in much the same way that Mandela and his most trusted lieutenants had done after the launch of their own armed struggle in 1960. In another ironic echo of the past, Mandela regarded Viljoen in the same way Viljoen had always regarded him, as a terrorist. Or, at any rate, as a terrorist in waiting. The difference was that Viljoen's forces were far more professional and had far more destructive potential than Umkhonto we Sizwe ever had.

Mandela could have used his growing authority to deploy the full might of the state security apparatus against Viljoen in the same way that it had been used against him three decades earlier. Grounds to arrest Viljoen for treason, for mounting an armed uprising against the state, were compelling. But Mandela knew that, in the best of cases, such a decisive action would mean making a martyr of Viljoen, and no one understood better than Mandela what the consequences of that would be. A far greater and more present danger was the possibility of the military mutinying in defense of a man regarded by many serving officers as a South African hero. So, Mandela fought back on the terrain that he knew best. Through secret channels, he invited General Viljoen to sit down and talk.

Thirteen years later, I would sit down and talk to him myself. Viljoen picked up the story for me at the rather unexpected venue he chose for our conversation: a hamburger joint at Camps Bay, a beautiful oceanside spot just outside Cape Town. But he asked me to meet him first at another address. It was at a place called Bakoven, also on the sea, barely a minute's drive away from Camps Bay. By the entrance to the house, at the end of a short cul de sac, stood a sign that read

"El Alamein." Appropriately named in memory of a famous battle in the Second World War in which South African forces fought alongside the British against Hitler's army, El Alamein was a small holiday home shared by retired army officers.

Viljoen was as stiff in his bearing as if he were inspecting troops on parade. While his manner was cautious he was not unfriendly, and decidedly not discourteous. His wife, on the other hand, was a charmer. Elegant and amiable, she spoke English as if it were her native tongue. Viljoen spoke in a more labored manner, with a hard Afrikaan accent. She came across as a carefree soul, at peace with Mandela's new South Africa. As for her husband, I was not so sure. It was intriguing, nevertheless, to be in domestic surroundings with Viljoen, cutting into the beach vacation of someone whom I had pictured as a dangerous fanatic. At speeches and press conferences, he would warn that armed action was on the way, that Mandela should bear in mind the anger among the Afrikaner people, that things in South Africa were about to spin out of control.

Yet, when he began describing to me his first encounter with Mandela he spoke with restraint, tautly measuring his words, oblivious to the music shaking the walls of the hamburger bar. Their meeting had taken place in September 1993 at Mandela's home in a prosperous residential area of Johannesburg that had historically been reserved, under apartheid's Group Areas Act, for whites only. Viljoen showed up at Mandela's door, he told me, along with three other retired generals. Between them, they made up the Volksfront directorate.

"I had expected a servant to come to the door but it was Mandela himself who greeted us," Viljoen said. "He was smiling as we shook hands, saying how happy he was to see us." Viljoen did not himself smile as he recalled the encounter. In fact, he only smiled once during the hour we spent together.

But even now, so long after the fact, he was unable to disguise the surprise he felt at Mandela's warm and courtly demeanor.

"After inviting us in, Mr. Mandela suggested he and I should have a separate conversation before our delegations formally sat down at the table," Viljoen continued. "I accepted and we went into his lounge. He asked me if I took tea. I said yes and he poured me a cup. He asked me if I took milk. I said yes and he poured me milk. Then he asked me if I took sugar with my tea. I said I did and he poured the sugar. All I had to do was stir it!"

That was the only moment in our interview when Viljoen said anything that justified an exclamation mark. It was, by his restrained conversational standards, an expression of utter amazement, and it told me practically all I needed to know about the effect Mandela had had on him.

Then, the general told me, the conversation changed gears, Mandela demonstrating that ability of his to switch instantly from light pleasantry to deadly seriousness. He pointed out to the general that, yes, he could take the route of war and, yes, he understood his people's fears and concerns. But it was a war which no one could win, and from which South Africa could only lose—while Viljoen's forces would be militarily more adept, Mandela's would count on greater numbers and the unanimous support of the international community. In the end, the only possible outcome would be the peace of the graveyards. The general did not disagree. His people, the Afrikaners, had always prided themselves on being what they called "survivors" in a hostile African continent. Mandela understood that part of Afrikaner nature, too and, by appealing to it in lawyerly argument, he succeeded in establishing the rational basis on which secret talks between the two men and their delegations would proceed in the weeks ahead.

Mandela captivated the general. What stayed with Viljoen from that first meeting was not so much the nitty-gritty of the political exchanges as what he called Mandela's "very respectful attitude." It was in Mandela's body language on greeting him, in the serving of the tea, and it was in something Mandela remarked to the general which he said made a deep impression on him, for it revealed, as he chose to see it, a keen understanding of Afrikaner values.

"Mandela began by saying that the Afrikaner people had done him and his people a lot of harm," General Viljoen recalled, "and yet somehow he had a great respect for the Afrikaners. He said that maybe it was because, though it was hard to explain to outsiders, the Afrikaner had a humanity about him. He said that if the child of an Afrikaner's farm laborer got sick, the Afrikaner farmer would take him in his *bakkie* [his four-wheel drive truck] to the hospital, phone to check up on him, and take his parents to see him. At the same time, an Afrikaner will be a demanding employer, Mandela said, but he was also human and that aspect of the Afrikaner was something Mandela was very impressed by."

I asked myself whether Mandela himself fully believed in this Good Samaritan portrait he painted of the Afrikaner farmer, but the general had not doubted Mandela's sincerity for one moment. I could see with perfect clarity that Mandela's words had struck home. They had soothed the general's vanity, corroborating the Afrikaners' idealized vision of themselves. The fact that Mandela had been balanced in his appraisal, that he had not spared the general a raw acknowledgment of the damage the Afrikaners had done to him and his people, only reinforced the general's conviction that Mandela was speaking his mind frankly and honestly. Was that manipulation? Was that Mandela striving deliberately to bend the general to his will?

Mandela was always a politician first and foremost, yet he did feel a genuine esteem and respect for the Afrikaners, whom unlike more radical black leaders, he regarded as genuine sons of the South African soil. In flattering the general's people, he probably believed, at that precise moment, what he was saying. But on another level, and quite possibly without fully realizing it, he was following the example of Abraham Lincoln, about whom he had read in prison—he was appealing to the better angels of General Viljoen's nature. He cut through their political disagreements and sought to draw out the best of the human being within. By highlighting the decency he had seen in Afrikaner farmers toward their laborers, he stressed the common humanity that bound all people together, undercutting core apartheid ideas to which the general's followers still seemed to cling. General Viljoen felt better about himself when he left that first meeting with Mandela than when he had gone in. The president of the United States then, Bill Clinton, would later recognize that was precisely the impact Mandela had on him. "He inspires us all to be the best human being we can possibly be," Clinton said.

Mandela also understood that the primary impulses that had led to the formation of the Afrikaner Volksfront were guilt and fear. Viljoen conceded as much in our conversation when he said, "We were very scared that if we gave away all the power, the Afrikaners would be flushed by the majority." He and his followers knew deep down that, for all their bluster, they had treated black people badly and so feared a proportionate revenge. Mandela's words and actions in that first meeting with Viljoen sought to ease that guilt and appease the fear. It worked.

"Mandela wins over all who meet him," Viljoen confessed. I immediately thought of an observation that Niel Barnard, apartheid's last head of national intelligence had made to me once. "Mandela," said Barnard, as studious an observer of Mandela's character as anyone alive, "has an almost animal instinct for tapping into people's vulnerabilities and reassuring them." The general's words, almost a concession of surrender, also reminded me of something Mandela had said to me once about how the way to reach white South Africans was by addressing not so much their brains as their hearts. I quoted that to Viljoen and then I asked him if he perhaps regarded Mandela's ability to conquer people that way as a form of genius? Made slightly uncomfortable by the question, suggesting as it did a certain weakness in his military self, the general did not, however, disagree. "Yes," he conceded, after a slight pause. "That is true. That is correct."

Mandela had also spoken to the general during that first meeting, and always afterward, in Afrikaans. For Viljoen, the mere fact of hearing Mandela speak to him in his native tongue was in itself immensely significant. The message he received was that if Mandela expressed respect for Afrikaans culture it was highly unlikely he would endeavor, as he and his followers had feared, to blot it off the face of the earth. Mandela knew exactly what he was doing—taking the first steps towards disarming the white far right. And he did it on the understanding, absorbed in prison, that in politics, as in war, the first rule is to know your enemy.

Prison taught Mandela realism. Black South Africans were not going to achieve democracy by fighting; they were going to do so by talking. Even though he had been sentenced to life in jail, somehow he knew, or perhaps had to believe, that one day he would be released, and one day he would lead his people to freedom. But, before doing so, he would have to win over the likes of General Viljoen. Learning Afrikaans was one of the first tasks he set himself on arrival in prison, to the consternation of some of his fellow political prisoners.

Fikile Bam, who was on Robben Island with Mandela from 1964 to 1975, told me during an interview we did in 1999, that he and the other inmates in B Section, the maximum security wing for political prisoners, could not understand at first why Mandela had decided to take a course in "the oppressor's language." They talked amongst themselves in English or in their tribal languages, such as Zulu or Xhosa, the one Mandela grew up speaking. To learn Afrikaans was, surely, to capitulate to the enemy. Mandela, who was looking far ahead into the future, did not pay them any attention. Eventually, Bam would tell me many years later, the rest of the prisoners got his point.

"Nelson was very serious about his Afrikaans," said Bam, a sober-minded man who would become a judge after Mandela came to power. "And not just the language, but he was very serious about learning to understand the Afrikaner—his mind and how he thought. Because in his mind, and he actually preached this, the Afrikaner was an African. He belonged to the soil and whatever solution there was going to be on the political issues, would have to involve Afrikaans people. They, after all, were part of the land . . . they had grown up and they had a history in the country, which he wanted to understand. . . . So, he studied very hard and the sort of things he studied were things which were obviously going to be of assistance in the future South Africa, in the actual political negotiations, which subsequently happened."

Mandela took a two-year correspondence course in Afrikaans and then set about reading Afrikaans history, paying special attention to the Anglo-Boer War, which, though the Afrikaners lost, was the decisive moment in their history. For the first time, the settlers of Dutch and French origin who had scattered across southern Africa felt a sense of common nationhood. Mandela made a point of learning the names and exploits of the Afrikaner heroes of that war, which would serve him well later when he spoke of them with knowledge and admiration in his meetings with Viljoen and other Afrikaner leaders. He also familiarized himself in prison with Afrikaans literature. When he made a request to the prison authorities to furnish him with the complete works of a celebrated Afrikaans poet called D. J. Opperman, they happily acceded.

To be able to put himself in the shoes of the enemy and to internalize their concerns would give him an advantage over them when the time came to sit down and talk. He used his studies and readings to get a sense of the vanities and points of pride of his enemies, where they were strong and where they were weak. More useful still was his relationship with his jailers, whom he got to observe closely, until the point came when Robben Island became a laboratory for his experiments in political persuasion, and the jailers his guinea pigs. As with General Viljoen, he set about his task with a seamless blend of pragmatism, political vision, and genuine decency.

Mandela explained as much in his autobiography. First the pragmatism: "The most important person in any prisoner's life is not the minister of justice, not the commissioner of prisons, not even the head of prison, but the warder in one's section. If you are cold and want an extra blanket, you might petition the minister of justice, but you will get no response. . . . But if you approach the warder in your corridor, and you are on good terms with him, he will simply go to the stockroom and fetch a blanket."

Then the decency and the political vision: "I always tried to be decent to the warders in my section; hostility was self-defeating. There was no point in having a permanent enemy among the warders. It was ANC policy to try to educate all people, even our enemies: we believed that all men, even prison service warders, were capable of change, and we did our utmost to try to sway them."

Mandela's autobiography, as well as Anthony Sampson's authorized biography, offers plenty of detail on how Mandela became the king of the island. As Sampson put it, he not only reversed the relationship between warder and prisoner, but came to dominate the prison. One of his lawyers from the 1964 trial, George Bizos, revealed how Mandela began to stamp his authority and his charm on the prison almost as soon as he had arrived.

"On my first visit, in the middle of winter 1964, he was brought to the consulting room where I was waiting," Bizos told me. "There were eight warders with him, two in front, two at the back, two on each side. Prisoners do not usually set the pace at which they move with their warders. But it was quite obvious that he was—from the open van that they came in, right up to the little veranda of the consulting rooms. And I stepped down, past the two in front, and embraced him, said, 'Hello.' He returned the greeting and immediately asked, 'How's Zami?' And he then pulled himself back, and said, 'George, I'm sorry, I have not introduced you to my guard of honor.' And then proceeded to introduce each one of the warders by name. Now, the warders were absolutely amazed. I think that this was the first time that they saw a white man, and particularly a lawyer, I suppose, coming and embracing a black man, but they were absolutely stunned, and they actually behaved like a guard of honor. They respectfully shook my hand."

I spent many hours talking with Christo Brand, a prison guard with whom Mandela forged a close friendship in jail. Brand formed such an attachment to Mandela that when he was offered a promotion that would have meant moving to another prison in 1984, he turned it down. "Mandela said to me, 'You know, Mr. Brand, if you leave we will lose a friend,'" Brand recalled. "And I thought, I will lose a friend too. So I stayed, till 1988. Nelson Mandela was very happy I stayed."

Brand was brought up in such poverty that he did not have electricity at home until he was six. He told me that Mandela used to berate him for not studying. "He used to say that I had a good mind and I was wasting my opportunities in life. He once wrote a letter to my wife urging her to get me to work harder so I would improve myself." Brand returned Mandela's kindness, and not only in terms of providing him with extra blankets and other small comforts. Once, he did Mandela a favor that had no price. One of the sorrows of prison life for Mandela was never having the opportunity of contact with children. One day in 1985, twenty-three years into Mandela's prison term, he gave Mandela his chance. Brand and his wife had had their first child, Riaan, eight months earlier. Brand smuggled the child into the prison and into Mandela's cell. "He took Riaan in his arms and he loved it. I think I saw tears in his eyes."

It was the memory of that gesture and others like it that explained what would become the most memorable statement to emerge from the press conference Mandela gave on the morning after his release. Explaining why any bitterness he might have felt had been wiped out, he said, "in prison there have been men who were very good in the sense that they understood our point of view and that they did everything to try and make you as happy as possible." Christo Brand would have been uppermost in his mind when he said that, though Mandela modestly neglected to add that if his jailers were attentive to him it was because his own behavior elicited that kindness in them.

Much the same could be said of his first encounters in prison with President P. W. Botha's two most trusted lieutenants: the minister of justice, Kobie Coetsee, and the intelligence chief, Barnard. The government's agreement to hold secret exploratory talks with him in prison represented a moment of triumph. It did not quite unlock the door to his cell, but it did open the way for the historic breakthroughs that would follow. Coetsee met with Mandela a dozen times prior to his release in February 1990, Barnard more than sixty.

Coetsee, who was South Africa's minister of justice between 1980 and 1993, was a small man whose place as a trusted member of the P. W. Botha court owed more to the fawning obsequiousness he showed the Big Crocodile than to any great intellectual merit or originality of thought. He fancied himself a bit of a classicist, and enjoyed flaunting his knowledge of Ciceronian discourse among his decidedly unlearned cabinet colleagues.

Barnard, by contrast, was the man in the presidential inner circle whose opinions Mandela listened to with greatest interest. Botha's very own eminence grise, Barnard was head of the National Intelligence Service between 1980 and 1992. He was tall, lean, pale, and somehow featureless, a man you would not remember if you came across him three times in a day. He left no trace, seemed to leave no shadow. He was the image of the perfect spy. I spent some six hours in his company in total, and the sense I had was not so much that I was talking to a blank wall as that a blank wall was talking to me.

During the time Mandela met with them in prison, Barnard and Coetsee were two of the most loathed and despised figures among black South Africans. They did not decide to meet Mandela as a consequence of any moment of moral awakening; they were not even well disposed towards him. They met him because the combination of rising national and international pressure had painted them into a corner, as Coetsee put it to me, and the time had come at least to explore political possibilities beyond violent repression. One might have expected, at best, an atmosphere of mutual wariness between them in their initial encounters, one that reflected the atmosphere in South Africa at large. The black townships were staging daily battles between activists and police, a state of emergency had been imposed, and Botha's government was jailing tens of thousands of activists without charge and, in some cases, authorizing political assassinations. Mandela, once again, controlled his emotions. A dynamic had been unleashed which he could do nothing to stop. Here a new, possibly history-changing dynamic presented itself to him and would be irresponsible to pass up. He could not waste this golden opportunity to initiate a process of political change by issuing demands that he knew would not be met.

What Mandela did instead was deploy his finely honed armory of political skills, personal charm, and keen knowledge of the Afrikaner mentality to set in motion a chain of events leading to the liberation of his people. The first goal was to establish a relationship of respect and trust with Coetsee and Barnard. He achieved that and, in time, even secured their affection.

Coetsee met him for the first time in the hospital, just after Mandela had undergone a prostate operation. Coetsee was in a dark suit; Mandela wore pajamas, a dressing gown, and slippers. When Barnard met him, he was in prison overalls and rubber boots. Appearances counted for little. Each time, Mandela wore the air of a head of state receiving the credentials of a foreign ambassador.

Both Coetsee and Barnard told me when I spoke to them more than a decade later that they each departed their first meeting with Mandela convinced he would one day become president of South Africa.

"He was a natural and I realized that from the moment I met him," Coetsee said. "He was a born leader, he was affable. . . . The first time I met him, I already saw him as president."

"Even in overalls and boots, he had a commanding kind

of presence and personality," Barnard recalled. "At that stage I already expected him to become most certainly the president of the country."

Embarrassed by the difference in their dress, the two servants of the apartheid state, both of them in effect Mandela's jailers, arranged for him to wear a suit at all subsequent meetings. The discussions were conducted in a climate of high seriousness, for the very future of their country—tyranny or democracy, peace or war—was the subject on the agenda. As Coetsee told it, "It all came very naturally to him, very affably, but underneath you sensed the ability to assert himself at the drop of a hat. It was always there. And that makes for good authority. There was a lot of humor, but we could and he could switch to business just like that." It was business far more than pleasure when Mandela met Coetsee and Barnard, but the more the two men got to know Mandela the more hopelessly they became ensnared in the web of his irresistible charm.

"I have studied the classics, and for me," said Coetsee, shedding tears as he spoke, "he is the incarnation of the great Roman virtues, gravitas, honestas, dignitas. Everywhere and anywhere, where people choose people, you can't help choosing Mandela." Barnard was the coldest of cold fish, but Mandela teased out of him a kernel of warmth that maybe even he did not know he possessed. During the six hours or so that I spent with him, he never mentioned Mandela by his name. He referred to him always as "the old man," as though he were talking about his father, or a favorite uncle.

By the time the secret talks between Mandela and his jailers ended, the prisoner had accomplished all of his objectives: his own release and that of other senior political prisoners, like his old friend Walter Sisulu, coupled with a government commitment to start a formal, public process of negotiations.

General Viljoen took less time to succumb. He was bewil-

dered by what he described as Mandela's "decency and polite-
ness" the first time they met, and over subsequent meetings,
his faith in Mandela only grew. "That first impression Mandela made on me made it less difficult later for me to make
my decision," Viljoen told me. "The important thing when you
negotiate with an enemy is the character of the people you have
across the table from you and whether they carry their people's
support with them: Mandela had both."

There was one particular initiative Mandela proposed
early in 1994 that went a long way towards convincing Viljoen
to throw up the white flag of surrender. On the delicate matter of what South Africa's new national anthem would be once
democracy was in place, Mandela had prevailed upon the otherwise dubious leadership of the national executive committee
of the ANC. The majority view initially had been that the old
white anthem, a martial tune celebrating the white conquest
of Africa's southern tip, would be scrapped and replaced by
"Nkosi Sikelel' iAfrika," the official song of black liberation.
Mandela chastised his fellow leaders, expressing shock at the
carefree way in which they proposed to stamp all over a symbolic piece of music that carried within it the identity and pride
of a sector of the South African population whose goodwill
was essential in order for the new experiment in democracy to
succeed. He suggested that the two anthems be kept and that
henceforth, in a proper spirit of national unity, one should be
sung after the other. Mandela, who had learned his prison les-
sons well, carried the day.

"Mandela," Viljoen said, "is a man with a very great sense
of responsibility. When he said to me, 'I want to be not an
ANC president but a president to the whole country,' he meant
it." Six months after the first meeting between the two men
the general had became sufficiently convinced by Mandela's
character and leadership to make what he said was the tough-

est decision of his life: ordering his followers to call off armed action. The repercussions of the general's decision were immense. Exactly how serious armed action would have been was revealed some years later when some of his men confessed before the Truth and Reconciliation Commission that plans had been well advanced for a nationwide terror campaign. A handful of militarily trained men under Viljoen's leadership could have plunged the country into chaos.

But Viljoen did not stop at calling off a war he had described to his followers less than a year earlier as both "bloody" and "inevitable." Capitulating entirely to Mandela's wishes, he took the enormous step of announcing, early in March 1994, that he would take part in the next month's elections. No peace agreement was worth more. In return for zero political concessions, persuaded almost entirely by the strength of Mandela's character, he gave his blessing to the entire process of democratic change, against which he had vowed only ten months earlier to fight to the death. Buthelezi, his alliance with the white men and their guns now over, found himself alone, with no choice but to call off Inkatha's own twisted variation on black armed struggle and, at the very last minute, join the elections, too. Later, he joined the coalition government, to which Mandela named him minister of home affairs.

Buthelezi was, at the time of his concession, the most hated man in South Africa. Black people were far more prepared to forgive the likes of Viljoen, who at least had been defending what he genuinely perceived to be the interests of white South Africa. But Mandela, as ever, when critical decisions of state were involved, opted for cold-blooded pragmatism. The long term stability of South Africa was best served having the Zulu chief inside the tent rather than out. There was a price to be paid in terms of efficient governance, but Mandela judged it was worth paying if the reward was an end to the killings. Buthelezi exercised his responsibilities as minister of home affairs with predictable incompetence, but he remained consistently meek as a lamb, his paranoid terrors having been finally tamed.

Viljoen praised Mandela's ability to carry his people with him, but he himself was less successful. He could not manage to take all of the Volksfront faithful on the road to peace. Only 50 percent of those who had appointed him their leader at Potchefstroom went along with his decision to participate in the elections. But, knowing his people's fearful mood and how difficult it had been to convince them of Mandela's bona fides, he considered 50 percent to be a success. Terrorist attacks by the remnants of the white far right did take place; bombs did go off, taking innocent black lives, in the final weeks before the April 27, 1994, election. Viljoen believed that if he had not made the decision he had, it would have been well within his leadership capabilities—"We had a plan in place," he said—to have severely disrupted the vote and possibly reduced South Africa's historic day to bloody anarchy.

In May 1994, Mandela was inaugurated as president, and a new parliament was opened that reflected the entire rainbow spectrum of races and religions in South Africa; two-thirds of the parliamentarians belonging to the ANC. Viljoen managed to win a seat, too, his party having picked up, he said, a third of the Afrikaner vote.

I was there at the opening of parliament, and I remember Mandela walking into the packed multicolored chamber where only gray-faced white men in suits had sat before. I noticed that Viljoen, standing at ground level, was staring at Mandela, transfixed.

Sitting with him in the hamburger bar in Camps Bay twelve years later, I suggested that the expression I saw on his face that morning evinced deep respect and affection. Uncomfortable, he answered with a curt, "Yes, that would be correct," but then he warmed to the theme. "Mandela came in and he saw me and he came across the floor to me, which he was not really supposed to do according to parliamentary protocol. He shook my hand and he had a big smile on his face and said how happy he was to see me there."

Then, and only then, for the first and last time in our meeting, Viljoen smiled. He had remembered something. "Suddenly, as we were shaking hands, a black voice from high up in the gallery shouted, 'Give him a hug, general!' " I was almost afraid to ask what he did.

"I am a military man and he was my president," the general answered, "I shook his hand and I stood to attention."

On the short drive back to his beach residence, I reflected on how different my perception of the general was from the time I first came across him at that night of the Afrikaner rally in Potchefstroom. He was, I had discovered, what de Klerk had been for Mandela on the day after his release: a man of integrity. He had been fixed in his ideas most of his life, but had had the moral courage to adapt and allow himself to change his mind. I asked him what he was doing now. He said he had quit politics five years earlier and gone back to his farm, the one he had left when he answered the call to lead his people to war in May 1993. Had he seen Mandela recently? "I saw him many times when he was president. His door was always open to me to discuss matters regarding the welfare of the Afrikaner. And I did see him again after I left politics. But I have not seen him recently because of reports that he is not in good health."

Would he like to see him again? We were about to shake hands and say good-bye. He permitted himself a small glimmer of emotion. "Yes, I would," he replied. "I would love to see him, though I do not wish to impose. But, yes, yes. I would love to see him again. He is the greatest of men."

# A HERO TO HIS VALET

Zelda la Grange entered Nelson Mandela's life when she was twenty-three and he was seventy-six; they remained inseparable for the rest of his days. She rose to become his personal assistant during his presidency, and when he retired from politics she continued working by his side, helping him administer his various charities. She accompanied him on nearly one hundred trips, organizing every detail of his schedule, attending to his dietary needs and other domestic comforts, playing the role of secretary, butler, aide-de-camp, spokesperson, protector, and confidante, chatting to him about matters public and private during the innumerable meals they shared, growing ever closer to him as the years went by. No one spent more time in his company than she for the remainder of his life after he became president. There were few people he trusted more, or for whom he felt greater affection. She called him *kuhlu*, which means "grandfather" in Mandela's Xhosa language.

A tall, busy, energetic blonde, she could be taken as an exemplary specimen of the Afrikaner master race. From afar, she comes across as forbidding and cold. When you get to know her, you realize that her aloofness is a requirement of her job as Mandela's gatekeeper, and that, once she drops her guard, she is funny, irreverent, plain speaking and, having met an abundance of Hollywood actors and heads of state, not at all easily impressed. She is as good a guide as any in helping answer the question I raise: whether Mandela was a cold manipulator, a consummate actor whose affability and goodness were guilefully put on. Was he less decent and kind in private than he made out to be in public? Did he have, in common with some other heroes of history, a dark side?

Zelda first met Mandela in August 1994, four months after Mandela had become president, and two weeks into her new job at the Union Buildings as a junior member of the secretarial typing pool. She ran into Mandela on her way into his secretary's office to fetch a document. "He started speaking Afrikaans to me, which I didn't understand immediately because the last thing I expected was for him to speak in my own language to me," Zelda would recall in a conversation we had fourteen years later in London, where elaborate celebrations were under way for Mandela's ninetieth birthday. "His Afrikaans was perfect but I was in such a state that I didn't understand what he was saying. I was shivering." She burst out laughing at the recollection. "Yes, shivering! I was scared of him, not knowing what to expect of him, whether he was going to dismiss me, humiliate me . . . and instantly it was that feeling of guilt that all Afrikaners carry with them."

Zelda insisted that, yes, all Afrikaners carried guilt within, even typical ones like herself and her family who had regarded themselves as apolitical. Her parents were God-fearing Pretoria folk who had always voted reflexively for the governing National Party, which ruled without interruption, inventing, and then enforcing apartheid, from 1948 to 1994. Zelda never gave a thought to politics as she grew up. Her contact with black people was limited to the live-in family maid, who, abiding by the rules of those times, uncomplainingly drank from separate cups, and used different knives and forks. Zelda thought nothing of it, though she did recall hearing President Botha announcing the imposition of a state of emergency on the radio and suddenly feeling afraid, as all white people at the time did, she said, that hordes of angry black people were going to rampage through her home in the middle of the night. The Afrikaners had a term for it, "swart gevaar," the black danger.

So, they didn't follow the details of the revolt in the townships, of the international protests, of their government's response but, in a way that they preferred not to reflect on, they knew that what they were doing to black people was unfair. The guilt was always lurking there somewhere, Zelda said, whether people admitted it or not. At that first face-to-face meeting with Mandela, all her own guilt was concentrated on what her people had done to him. "You could see he wasn't sixty, he was seventy-six at the time, and you could see he was old and the thing that immediately crosses your mind is, 'I sent this man to jail! My people sent this man to jail!' I was part of this even though I couldn't vote. I was part of this, of taking from a person like him his whole life away. And then I started crying."

Zelda gave the impression that she would not have been surprised if he had slapped her face. But, however warranted Zelda might have felt such a response to have been, his impulse was quite different. "He shook my hand and then he held it. I was very emotional, shedding tears. I didn't know what to do. I'd never met any president in my life. But he just held my hand and he continued to speak to me, still holding my hand, and then when he saw I was still so emotional, he put his other hand on my shoulder and said, 'No, no, no . . . this is not necessary, you're overreacting a bit.' I settled down, maybe smiled at that, and then he started asking me questions. Where had I grown up? What did my parents do? We ended up talking for about five minutes. But it wasn't special treatment he was giving me. He would talk to all members of the staff, black and white, in the same way when he met them, asking them about their backgrounds and their families."

I spoke to another member of the presidential staff, another Afrikaner, and found that there was a pattern here. His name was John Reinders. He reported for work the morning after Mandela's inauguration, on May 11, 1994, convinced he would be fired along with all the rest of the white staff. He was mistaken. No sooner had Mandela arrived, Reinders told me, than he called a meeting of all the employees and, after introducing himself to each of them, and asking them where they were from, he begged them all to stay, saying he needed their expertise because he and his people had no clue how a presidential office should be run. "Now, this is not an order," Mandela said. "I want you here if you wish to stay and share your knowledge and your experience with me." They all stayed.

I spoke to Reinders at his office in the Union Buildings in 2006. He had remained with Mandela until the end of his presidential term in 1999, then stayed on with his successor, Thabo Mbeki. Reinders was candid, a massive, hard-muscled human who in his youth had to have been a formidable rugby player. He shook my hand with his left when we met because, as he explained, he had broken his right after punching a wall in a rage after his staff had failed to meet his deadline for some ceremonial arrangement. Jovial, polite, about fifty years old, he said that in 1980 he had been working as a major in the prison service when Botha summoned him to work in the presidency. There he remained, continuing on with de Klerk, until Mandela took over. "P.W. called me 'major,' F.W. called me nothing, and Nelson Mandela called me 'John'," Reinders said, adding with a smile: "I think that says it almost all."

Recalling how he and Mandela would often banter about their shared experience in the prison service, he said that the entire staff at the Union Buildings, white and black, were "mesmerized" by him.

"We were all eating out of his hand from the day we met him, from the first day to the last. As a matter of routine, he'd walk in to my office and other people's and say, 'How are you today?' If staff members had relatives who were sick, he would always remember to ask how they were doing. When a secretary had worked with me in the presidency for several years had an accident he sent her flowers. He made time for everybody."

One of Reinders' jobs was to go into Mandela's office at eight-fifteen in the morning with the morning papers. "He always stood up when I came in. Every single time." As for the finer points of protocol, Reinders said Mandela flouted the rules if he felt they came into conflict with his notion of good manners. Accompanying Mandela once on a visit to Rome, Reinders found himself standing just behind his boss when he greeted the Pope. Mandela then turned around and, with a large smile, introduced him to Reinders, with whom the surprised Pontiff had no choice but to shake hands too.

The big man's eyes brimmed with tears when he told me of an encounter at the end of 1994 between Mandela and Reinders' wife, Cora. He invited both of them to his residence for a Christmas barbecue along with other members of staff. "He saw Cora and he greeted her very warmly," Reinders said, "and then he put his arm around my shoulder and said to her. 'Where did you find this remarkable man?' My wife was so moved she couldn't breathe."

There is a saying that no man is a hero to his valet. Man-

dela and John Reinders were an exception to the rule. So were
Mandela and Zelda la Grange. Zelda insisted to me that there
was nothing that she disliked about him, not even the fact that
he often had to take phone calls at one or two in the morning
as president or that she always, at all hours, had to be by his
side. Nor was she bothered by his obsession with punctuality.

"He is a stickler for that," she said. "He does not like to
waste other people's time. He really dislikes it when people
come in late for meetings and he is very uncomfortable when
he is late, even if it's for reasons he cannot control." The habit
of punctuality for him was not merely a matter of good manners, Zelda explained, it was an expression of the importance
he attached to showing respect for others. He had no higher
value.

I once asked Mandela's friend and political mentor, Walter
Sisulu, if he could sum up what exactly it was Mandela had
been fighting for all his life. He replied far more simply than
I had expected. "Ordinary respect," he said. That was all, no
more no less. Apartheid had been the opposite of ordinary
respect—it had been an expression of extraordinary contempt.
Once respect became the norm of social exchange between
people of all races, it would mean apartheid had gone. Being
punctual, Mandela figured, was a good starting point—even
towards us journalists, for whom the indignity of being kept
waiting by the high and mighty is part of the job. Whenever
circumstances beyond Mandela's control delayed the schedule
for a press conference, he would always begin the proceedings
with a profuse apology.

A skeptic might say that the courtesy Mandela displayed
towards the press, or to Zelda and John Reinders and the rest
of the presidential staff, never mind Viljoen, Kobie Coetsee or
Niel Barnard, had a self-serving, practical motive behind it.
Either he had a political objective in mind or he sought to en-

sure that the people who worked for him served him loyally. The same might be said of the large symbolic gestures he made to the old enemy after he became president, such as traveling hundreds of miles to have tea with Betsie Verwoerd, the aged widow of Hendrick Verwoerd, one of apartheid's founding fathers.

Verwoerd, who once famously said, "I never suffer from the nagging doubt that perhaps I might be wrong," was South Africa's prime minister between 1958 and 1966. In the liberation movement's pantheon of rogues, no one stood taller; he was the ideologue-in-chief of racial separation. It was during his time in office that Mandela opted to take up arms and that Mandela was jailed. Mandela returned the favor when it was his turn in office by paying his respects to his widow, whom he later invited to lunch along with the surviving wives of every other apartheid president or prime minister at the residence in Pretoria where they themselves had once lived.

No less astonishing was the lunch invitation he extended to Percy Yutar, the prosecution lawyer who had fought hard not just to convict Mandela, but to persuade the judge to sentence him to death. Mandela had the attentiveness not only to organize a kosher meal for Yutar, who was Jewish, but to apologize on the lawyer's behalf by noting in a public statement that he had only been doing his duty in his capacity as state prosecutor.

Certainly, Mandela had a clear political purpose with these deliberately staged acts of public forgiveness. He was sending a message to all his compatriots that said, "If I can do it, you can too." It was all part of what he called "nation building." He knew very well that much work remained to be done before the new South Africa project could be regarded as bulletproof. Some of General Viljoen's old loyalists remained on the loose, fearful and insecure. Mandela was also concerned

that destabilizing elements still remained within the old security police. Historic precedent in other countries in which
the old order had been dramatically overturned pointed to
the likely emergence of a counterrevolutionary terrorist force.
All it needed was a few dozen bomb-trained men with murder
in their hearts to put the entire project at risk. Defusing that
threat once and for all became a central mission of Mandela's
presidency. He had made it clear from the day of his inauguration that cementing the foundations of a fragile new democracy was the most important task that faced him. It was also
a job for which he was naturally suited, since it consisted of
making everybody feel they belonged in the new South Africa.
A political adviser of Mandela's in the presidency defined the
challenge well when he quoted Garibaldi as saying, "We have
made Italy. Now we must make Italians."

That included, in the South African case, the less belli-
cose English-speaking sector of the white community. While
the Afrikaners had, broadly speaking, run the apartheid state,
the English speakers had dominated the private economy. The
wealthiest South Africans tended to be the so-called English,
and they also tended to vote for the Democratic Party, the
most significant opposition party outside the coalition government that Mandela now headed. It had a tiny representation in parliament compared to the ANC, but nonetheless, the
DP's sharp and feisty leader Tony Leon, a lawyer half Mandela's age, got into the habit of giving Mandela a testing time
in parliamentary debate, probing relentlessly for weaknesses
in his administration, badgering him on matters of economic
and foreign policy

One day, Mandela had had enough. He said he was fed up
with being continually pestered by Leon's little Mickey Mouse
party. Leon delivered a typically caustic reply. "Yes, Mr. President, and the people of South Africa are fed up with your gov-

ernment's Goofy economics." Mandela took the reply in good spirits as the parliamentary chamber rolled with laughter. Barely a week later, Leon suffered a massive heart attack. He had a quadruple bypass operation at a hospital in Johannesburg. A few days later, Mandela went to the hospital to pay him a visit. Mandela approached Leon's room, saw he was awake and, before his parliamentary rival was aware of his presence, piped up, "Hello, Mickey Mouse. This is Goofy!"

Leon never forgot Mandela's gesture or the hearty laugh the two men shared. Mandela had struck the target—the leader of the opposition was transformed there and then into a devotee. Kindness, once again, with a purpose.

He worked his charm on the international stage, too, ensuring that South Africa evolved rapidly from being regarded as the world's pariah to everybody's darling. President Clinton admired him more than any other world leader. That was perhaps to be expected. More surprising was his wooing of the Queen of England. The closeness of his relationship with the most aloof head of state (or, at any rate, of a democratic state) on the planet, reached a point of such natural cordiality that, when he went on visits to London, even after leaving the presidency, Mandela would call her on leaving Heathrow airport, as one does with friends when one arrives in their hometown. Appointments between the two were naturally arranged ahead of time, but not always. When Mandela showed up one afternoon at Buckingham Palace for tea after checking in at his hotel, Queen Elizabeth asked him where he was staying. He said he was staying at the Dorchester. "Oh, no, Nelson," the Queen replied, "This is your Dorchester. Do come and stay with me." Whereupon Mandela instructed Zelda to arrange for his pajamas and toothbrush to be collected from his hotel and delivered to the palace, where he spent the night.

More remarkable still was the way he addressed her. A

friend of mine and his wife, John and Denise Battersby, were having lunch with him at his home in Johannesburg during the final year of his presidency. Suddenly a member of his staff walked into the dining room with a portable phone. The Queen of England was on the line. Mandela lit up, took the phone, and exclaimed, "Ah, hello, Elizabeth!" And then, "How are the boys?" referring to the princes William and Harry, whose mother, Diana, had recently died.

Mandela withdrew to the living room to proceed with the conversation in private. On his return he chuckled that his wife, Graça Machel, would complain to him that it was not right to call the Queen of England by her first name. His wife had a point. There was quite possibly no one alive, with the possible exception of the Queen's husband, who called her Elizabeth. In another age, it would have been a hanging offense. Mandela was a commoner, and from the colonies to boot, but I can only conclude that the affectionate ease she felt in his company was a consequence of that quality of natural majesty that many of us detected in him on first acquaintance.

Mandela was only an aristocrat in the most tenuous sense, tracing his line of descent to ancient Xhosa kings, yet the Queen of England found herself relating to him on an equal footing. They also shared a mission: they were both required to be unifying national figures.

The relationship between the two was perhaps not the most important reason why South Africa enjoyed excellent relations with the old imperial power during Mandela's presidency and beyond, but it certainly helped. South Africa is unlikely ever to have a more effective ambassador.

Yes, there was plenty of cold calculation behind the charm, but I do not believe that was all there was to it. As Archbishop Tutu said, "Does he calculate when he says I am going to visit Betsie Verwoerd? When he says I am going to have lunch with

Percy Yutar? I mean is it calculation? Is it spontaneous? Is it calculated?" Tutu's answer was "Yes and no." The line, he said, was very thin.

I believe that the line is so thin you cannot see it. The politician and the person blend naturally into one. Mandela's charm was second nature. His instinct was to be generous, decent, and polite, partly, no doubt, out of a need he shared with most of humanity, to be respected and loved. The instinct to be kind went hand in hand with the political imperative to woo the multitudes. One reinforced the other. He could be sincerely himself while at the same time aware that his natural mode of behavior served a political purpose. People in turn tapped instinctively into Mandela's sincerity, even if they were simultaneously aware that he had a political agenda. People never felt fooled by Mandela. After fighting my own journalistic impulse to doubt the good intentions of the powerful, I have found that I agree with Zelda la Grange and John Reinders that Mandela was decent for decency's sake.

The first time I really began to grasp the depth of the coherence between Mandela the politician and Mandela the private man was at the end of April 1994, just after he and the rest of the black population had cast the first votes of their lives in a national election. The story I was told was this: six weeks before the elections, John Harrison, BBC television's South Africa correspondent, had been killed in a car crash. An hour-and-a-half after the terrible news was made public the phone rang at Harrison's home. A friend of Harrison's wife, whose name was Penny, answered it. "Hello," the voice said. "This is Nelson Mandela. Could I speak to Mrs. Harrison, please?" The friend's first reaction was to assume this was a particularly tasteless prank call. But the man on the phone persevered and eventually persuaded her that he really was who he said he was.

It was a particularly frenetic time for Mandela. He was

in the middle of a nationwide election campaign while at the same time struggling to persuade Buthelezi's Inkatha and the white right to lay down their arms. But this was no perfunctory gesture, and certainly no vote-catching exercise. Mandela spoke to the newly widowed Penny for nearly a half hour. I learnt later that the conversation turned to Mandela's shared experience of such grief. He too had suffered the devastating loss of a loved one in a car crash. Mandela's eldest son, Thembi, had died in a road accident seven years after his father, whom he adored, had been imprisoned on Robben Island. A month later, at an ANC election rally in Zulu country, Mandela spotted Mrs. Harrison's friend among the journalists. He approached her and asked: "How's Penny doing?"

On a much lighter note, there was a story told to me by Tony O'Reilly, an Irish newspaper magnate who got to know Mandela well. "Mandela said he wanted a rest before the start of the election campaign and so I invited him to my place in the Bahamas," O'Reilly said. "For eight days at the end of 1993 he stayed there on his own, with two bodyguards, and I had a butler there, called John Cartwright, who fell in love with him, like everybody else does. John became devoted to him. Mandela said to me a few months later that he wanted to invite me to his presidential inauguration, and would I bring John Cartwright, too? And, sure enough, the invitations arrived, two for me and two for John. Unfortunately, I could not go. On the day itself I was in a pub in the United States watching the event on television. So I am sitting there watching and the TV commentator in typically stentorian American tones was saying 'We are watching one of the great scenes of political history, the presidential inauguration of Nelson Mandela, South Africa's first ever black leader and 400 of the world's leaders are here and the American delegation is led by First Lady Hillary Rodham Clinton and with her is vice president Al Gore and next to them is . . . is . . .' I'm thinking, 'No! Jesus Christ, it's John! Right there, tucked in with the American delegation . . . what a moment!' "

Mandela never forgot kindness shown to him. He remained loyal always to his jailer Christo Brand, an individual of no further practical use to him after he left prison, and to Brand's son Riaan, whom he had held when he was a baby in prison. Brand, a cheerful man who speaks of Mandela almost as if he were just another friend, told me that in prison Mandela would call him "Mr. Brand," and he would call Mandela, simply, "Nelson." The habit never wore off, even after Mandela became president, when Brand phoned him to offer his congratulations. Mandela had given him his home phone number, a detail Brand reported with as much matter-of-factness as when he happened to mention that they were together again in Amsterdam in 2002. "He introduced me to the Queen of Holland and I helped him up some stairs," Brand said.

Mandela invited Brand to his eightieth birthday party at the presidency in Pretoria in 1998, an event at which Mandela also announced his marriage to his third wife, the woman with whom he would finally discover lasting happiness, Graça Machel, the widow of the former president of Mozambique, Samora Machel, and previously minister of education in the Mozambican government. Mandela organized Brand's flight up from Cape Town—it was the first time he had been on a plane.

Mandela would fly down to see him seven years later. Mandela had been sending birthday cards to Riaan every year following his release from prison. As Riaan grew older, Mandela added notes urging him to be disciplined in his studies. When Riaan finished school, he helped him get access to a course in commercial sea-diving. "Mandela always told me that he considered Riaan to be a responsibility of his," Brand said.

Then, in December 2005, yet another car crash. Riaan was killed at age twenty-two. Christo Brand was at the morgue identifying his son's body when Mandela phoned him to offer his condolences and say he wished to fly down for the funeral. "But it was happening the very next day, and he could not make it down," Brand said. "So, soon after, he came down to Cape Town to visit me at home."

Mandela was also gratuitously kind to me. I wrote him a note the week I was leaving South Africa, early in 1995, after six years as a correspondent there. I sent the note by fax and, fifteen minutes later, I received a phone call from one of his secretaries at the Union Buildings asking me if I could make it to lunch with the president on Thursday, two days later. I said I could. She told me it would be an event at which fifty or so people would be present to celebrate the birthday of an old comrade-in-arms of Mandela, Yusuf Cachalia. I learned later from Cachalia's wife, Amina, that Mandela had phoned her prior to giving me the invitation, to make sure it was okay. When the time came for him to speak at the lunch he dwelt largely on his old friendship with Yusuf Cachalia, but he also found time to say one or two kind words about me.

It is redundant for me to say that I fell for his charm, but I take comfort in the knowledge that, as a journalist, I was hardly alone. I don't know any colleague, however experienced or otherwise cynical by nature, who did not fall for him, too. My friend Bill Keller, who was *New York Times* bureau chief when I was in South Africa, who had won a Pulitzer Prize for his work on the fall of the Soviet Union, and who later became executive editor of the *Times*, told me once in his office that of all the exalted political figures he had met in his life none had been in Mandela's league.

Zelda la Grange, who had much better reason than either of us to know, also said she had never met anybody remotely like him. She told me she loved his sense of humor, how more than any other of the great and the good she knew none put himself down in front of other people like Mandela, "but in a funny way." What was best about him, she said, was simple, really: "His humaneness. The way he is a very, very good human being. The question people most often ask is if there really is no bitterness and it's so easy to answer that: No! No crack has ever shown. If it was me who had suffered the way he did: No way! So, he is a special, extraordinary human being. So generous, and you see that in his interest in ordinary people. He really does want to know how your father or your mother or your brother is doing when he asks you." That was why she admired him, she said, but, more than that, why she loved him.

Love, or something very much like it, was what John Reinders felt for him, too. A year after Mandela had left the presidency, Reinders, who remained at the Union Buildings serving his successor, Thabo Mbeki, received a phone call—it was his former boss. Would he and his family be available for lunch at his home the following Sunday?

Reinders' tears streamed down his cheeks, as he told me how he and his wife showed up at Mandela's home in Johannesburg along with his two teenage children. He had expected them to form part of a large gathering but it was just John, his wife and children, and Mandela. "We sat down at the table but, before we started eating, President Mandela stood up and raised a glass. He addressed himself not to me but to my wife and children. He apologized to them for having got me to work so hard. He said he had deprived them far too often of the company of their husband and father. Then he looked at me and he looked at them again and said, 'But he was magnificent in the performance of his duties. Magnificent!' "

After lunch was over, Mandela accompanied the Reinders family to the door and escorted them to their car. "As we drove off," Reinders said, "he stood there waving at us with that beautiful big smile of his. We all waved back."

Why did he invite them to lunch and address that speech of apology and thanks to John Reinders' wife and children? Because he put into practice in private the values he proclaimed on the public stage, because far from the TV cameras in the intimacy of his home, without any consideration of self-interest or political gain, he was in the habit of being generous, respectful, courteous, and kind.

# 7

# WHITE TEARS

**O**ne fist in the air means defiance. Two fists means celebration. Mandela raised one when he left prison; he raised
two five and a half years later once the battle was truly won.
When he set out on his quest, he embodied the aspirations of
one sector of the most racially divided nation on earth; when
he completed it, he was the acknowledged leader of an entire
country. At the moment of triumph, a giant, blond Afrikaner
stood by his side, the two men a symbol of the moment when
South Africa became one country, at last.

The white man was Francois Pienaar, captain of the South
African rugby team, the Springboks. He woke up that day, in
the eyes of a people for whom rugby is a religion, as the captain of all Afrikaners—their spiritual leader, the individual in
whom their faith, hope, and collective pride were invested. By
the end of June 24, 1995, he was an even greater hero, but the
mantle of undisputed leadership had passed to Mandela. Johannesburg's Ellis Park rugby stadium, hitherto a cathedral
where only whites worshipped, became a monument to na-

tional unity when the Springboks triumphed, putting the final seal on Mandela's own victory on the South African stage.

The World Cup final of 1995 was much, much more than a game. It was a transcendent political event masquerading as a sporting contest. It was the happiest moment of Mandela's political life, the consummation of all his dreams. It was, as Archbishop Tutu, the ever-lucid chorus of the South African drama, put it, "a defining moment in the life of our country."

I told the story in a book called *Playing the Enemy*, which was made into the film *Invictus*, directed by Clint Eastwood. What I didn't do there was tell how full of laughter the two conversations I had with Mandela about the World Cup had been, nor how full of tears my interviews with the players and other Afrikaners had been. Since then, I've thought often about a challenge issued to me by one of the players, James Small. As we were saying good-bye, he said, "You see these tears. That's why you should write this book."

During my interview with Mandela, he made no effort to disguise the fact that he was pleased with himself. He knew he had pulled off an amazing tightrope act. Any ordinary politician, any ordinarily good and decent one, would have been filled with trepidation at the prospect of hosting an event as potentially divisive as the rugby World Cup, especially when stability remained far from assured. It used to be said of Yasser Arafat that he never missed an opportunity to miss an opportunity. Mandela, a politician who saw opportunities where others did not even know they existed, set himself the implausible task of transforming a sport that for decades had been a symbol of hatred and division into an instrument of national reconciliation.

I met with Mandela at his home in Johannesburg, in August 2001. Retired from the presidency for two years, he was eighty-three and of strong mind, but his legs were failing him.

This time, he did not stand up when I walked into his sitting room, but his greeting was as effusive as it had been when I interviewed him just after his inauguration. "Hello, John, hello! How are you? Very good to see you!" There was a woman serving tea then, too, whose entrance he celebrated, again interrupting his answer to one of my questions in midsentence, with as much gratitude and courtesy as he had shown Mrs. Coetzee at the Union Buildings. This time the woman was black.

Mandela winked at me as she left and, with a complicit smile, said, "You know, that lady, she is related to Chief Buthelezi."

"Oh, really," I replied, "what kind of relative?"

"She is married to a Buthelezi." I gave him a knowing smile back. Even that old foe was well and truly inside his tent now.

I began by asking how the idea came to him to use sport as a political instrument, given that sport had been another terrain in which races had been kept separate under apartheid. Rugby, and particularly the Springbok national team, had always been loathed by blacks as much as it had been a source of pride for whites.

Mandela replied that he had been aware for some time of the potential power sport had to generate a new, all-inclusive patriotism amongst all South Africans. "Once the negotiations started, I decided to mobilize sportsmen and -women and also the general public, especially blacks, to say to them, 'Up to now, sport has been the application of apartheid in the sports field, but now, things are changing. Let us strike a chord with the whites. Let us use sport for the purpose of nation building and promoting all the ideas which we think will lead to peace and stability in the country.' "

But rugby, he agreed, presented a unique difficulty. Under apartheid rules, a limited number of black people had been allowed to watch rugby games, and always in a strictly demarcated pen within the stadiums. The black fans always, unfailingly, supported the Springboks' rivals, booing when the all-white Springboks scored, celebrating raucously when their rivals did, no matter whether they were playing England, New Zealand, or Paraguay.

Mandela gave his blessing to hosting the rugby World Cup, a move correctly calculated as bait for the rugby-mad Afrikaners to go along with the new political dispensation, but he also sought to persuade black people to change the political habits of a lifetime and support the Springboks. "I knew that rugby generated great anger and hostility among blacks, but I decided to appeal to them and say these sportsmen in rugby are no longer our enemies. They are now our boys. We should embrace them. My idea was to ensure that we get the support of Afrikaners. And rugby, as far as Afrikaners are concerned, is a religion. But, you know, the response was very negative."

Mandela smiled to himself. He was not without vanity, most obviously in terms of his personal appearance. There were those glossy, brightly colored shirts he always wore in public after becoming president, made to his own specifications. He was, as his old friend and biographer Anthony Sampson used to say, "a bit of a showman, a bit of a dandy." In the fifties, when he was a struggling lawyer, he would have his suits made at the same tailor as South Africa's richest mining magnate. His vanity, I now saw for the first time, extended to his political triumphs. He would have been too shrewd and too polite to have rubbed his internal opponents' noses in their defeats, but I could only deduce, from his satisfied air, that privately he savored being in a position to say, "I told you so."

"You had a hell of an obstacle to overcome in persuading your people to back the Springboks," I said him.

"Oh, absolutely! Oh, it was very difficult," he replied, smil-

ing more broadly. A political rally with his own ANC supporters came to his mind. The rally took place in a rural Zulu town,
the day before South Africa played France in the semifinals of
the World Cup. Thousands were present.

"You know, John, they booed me. When I said these
Springbok boys are now ours, my own people booed me!"
Mandela was laughing now. Then he settled down and, more
seriously, described what happened next.

"I then had to harangue them and I said, look, 'Amongst
you are leaders, don't be shortsighted, don't be emotional. Nation building means that we have to pay a price, as well as the
whites have to pay a price. For them to open sports for blacks,
they are paying a price; for us to say we must now embrace the
rugby team is paying a price. That's what we should do.' And
now the booing calmed down. And I said: 'You are absolutely
emotional. I want leaders amongst you, men and women to
stand up and promote this idea.' And eventually, you know . . ."
he began to chuckle again, "eventually I got the crowd."

He had gobbled them up. By the end, they were cheering
him, as they had done in Katlehong two years earlier, when he
had threatened to quit as their leader unless they accepted his
call for peace.

The more remarkable thing about the rugby World Cup
was how he got the whites to cheer for him, too. He confessed
that this had surprised him, all the more so because his decision to support the Springboks had come in part as a response
to an urgent concern. Halfway through his first year as president, his intelligence people had got wind of a right-wing plot
headed by the unreconciled remnants of General Viljoen's old
followers "to topple the government," as Mandela put it. He
not only had to defuse that plot, but to create a national atmosphere in which such plots would never be hatched again. That,
he said, was where the rugby World Cup came in. "With the

Afrikaners," he explained, "you don't just address their brains, you address their hearts."

In doing the research for a documentary called *The 16th Man*, based on my book, *Playing the Enemy*, I also spoke to Koos Botha. For most of his life an archetypal Afrikaner of the far right, Botha was a terrorist—he had planted a bomb. Luckily, no one died. While Mandela was in jail in the seventies and eighties, Botha worked as a civil servant at the department that enforced the Separate Amenities Act, the one that prohibited black people from using the same public toilets, telephones, trains or buses as whites. For most of his life, he was a loyal servant of the National Party but deserted in the mid-eighties to the more unapologetically racist Conservative Party, after reaching the conclusion that his namesake President Botha was going soft on blacks. He became a Conservative Party member of parliament, raged when Mandela was released ("I never understood back then why they had not hanged him," he admitted to me) and raged still more when he discovered, early in 1991, that a school in Pretoria previously for whites only was going to take in the children of exiled ANC members. Impelled by a deep sense of duty, he went to the school one night in June that year and blew it up.

Not long after carrying out the bombing, he began to suspect that maybe he had been completely out of his mind. He was arrested and, while out on bail pending trial, he found himself taking part in a delegation of previously hard-line, but suddenly softening Afrikaner politicians invited to meet with Mandela. "He must have known about my background," Botha recalled, "yet there he was, so respectful, talking pleasantly to us in our own language."

Botha, choking back tears as he spoke, formed the same sort of impression of Mandela as Coetsee, Barnard, and Viljoen had after their first encounters with him. But being a

down-to-earth Afrikaner for whom actions spoke louder than
words, it took two concrete steps by Mandela to convince him
to throw in his lot with him. The first, he said, was Mandela's
decision to convince the national executive of the ANC to in-
corporate the old national anthem into the new. "That was a
moving gesture by him. That showed the man he was. It was
answering respect with respect. I even remember very soon
after he became president he was addressing a political gathering and the people there, who were mainly black people, were
singing only 'Nkosi Sikelele.' He stopped them and he forced
them to sing the Afrikaans version of the anthem, 'Die Stem.'
Those types of gestures made me lose my fighting spirit."

What clinched it for Koos Botha, however, was the rugby
World Cup final. He wasn't the only one. Mandela won over
practically the totality of the white population that day. As for
the Springbok players, winning that game was and would always remain their lives' most momentous achievement.

I'm not sure I have met anybody who worships Mandela
more than the Springbok captain Francois Pienaar. The first
time Pienaar met Mandela was a full year before the World
Cup. Mandela had invited him to the Union Buildings for tea.
Pienaar told me he felt more nervous going into that meeting
with him than he ever had piling into a rugby scrum. He said
his nerves eased within seconds of entering the presidential office. "It's more than just being comfortable in his presence,"
Pienaar told me, his eyes swelling with tears, "you have a feeling when you are with him that you are safe. As you would
with a wise and loving granddad."

Pienaar had not greeted Mandela's arrival at the presidency
with unfettered joy. He had been brought up in a typically un-
reflective pro–National Party home and, while generally aware
as he got older of the political issues in his country, rugby was
the only subject to which he devoted serious thought. Awed as

he might have been upon meeting Mandela, he was not pre-disposed to think like him, much less to act politically on his behalf. However, by the time he left the Union Buildings, his mission was clear: he and his teammates had to win the World Cup for South Africa and the old man.

Mandela had worked his magic again. When I spoke to him about that first meeting between them, I described the Springbok captain as a great big blond son of apartheid, the idealized image of Afrikaner might, to which he responded with another chuckle, "That is true! Absolutely! Absolutely!" When I reminded him of Pienaar's nerves before entering his office, he cracked up. But when I put it to him that he had in-vited Pienaar to tea in order to recruit him as a disciple to his national cause, he stopped laughing.

"I did that, yes," he replied. "I concentrated on compli-menting him for the role which he was playing and which he could play. And I briefed him on what I was doing about sports and why I was doing so. Francois, of course, was the captain of rugby and if I wanted to use rugby, I had to work with him. And I found him quite a charming fellow and an educated chap. He had a B.A. L.L.B. [in law], and it was a pleasure to sit with him. He is a remarkable chap."

Though not half as remarkable as Pienaar found Man-dela. The affection between the two men was genuine, but, whether Pienaar liked it or not, the fact was that Mandela had asked him to tea because he wanted to "use" rugby. Pienaar and his players allowed themselves to be used, responding as Mandela would have wished. They made high-profile visits to black townships to coach young children, made all the new South African noises in public and in private, and diligently learned the words of the black half of the national anthem. Mandela returned the compliment by visiting them at their training camp outside Cape Town just before the Springboks' first World Cup game in May 1995.

"I said to them," Mandela recalled, " 'You are playing the world champions: Australia. The team who wins this match will go right through the end.' And I said, 'You now have the opportunity of serving South Africa and uniting our people. From the point of view of merit, you are equal to anything in the world. But we are playing at home and you have got the edge. Just remember, all of us, black and white, are behind you.' "

Mandela made a point before the visit of memorizing all the players' names. The easiest to remember was Chester Williams, the one black player on the team. He was there on merit; no one grudged him his place. But he stood out in such a way as to highlight, if anything, just how white a sport rugby remained. Mandela, rather than make an issue of this, did not single out Williams for special attention. The message he conveyed to the players was that, no matter whether they were black or white, what counted now was that they were all equally legitimate and valued representatives of their country. When he went down the line greeting them one by one, like a general inspecting his troops, each was thrilled to be individually recognized by a man who was not only their president, but was also now a huge global celebrity. One thing they did understand, though, was that the Springbok emblem had always generated hostile feelings among Mandela's followers. Daringly, one of the players in the line handed Mandela a Springbok cap. Pienaar has the image of that moment fixed in his brain. "Immediately, without hesitation, he put it on his head. Without any hesitation whatsoever." By the time Mandela left, the Springboks understood they had a role to play in the life of their country bigger than they had ever imagined. They knew they were political players now. "He gave us a message," Pienaar recalled, "and we all understood it. This was bigger than just a game."

Mandela had embraced the old enemy; now he expected the old enemy to embrace him back.

James Small, who had a reputation as a wild man off the field, responded to Mandela's call with the zeal of a born-again convert. "It was kind of like we were his disciples," said Small. "He had touched us with his hand and said, 'Come on, let's have a go now.' And we had a go and there we were. We were his tools. He's a clever man. By the energy he gave us, he was our sixteenth man. Without him we wouldn't have won."

The Springboks beat Australia in the first game of the World Cup and, as Mandela predicted, they made it all the way to the final, grasping with ever greater wonder that Mandela had also been right about black South Africa lending them their support. "Our boys" were everybody's boys now.

For the first time since the arrival of the first white settlers in southern Africa in 1652, the black and white populations were united in one goal. The entire country longed for a Springbok victory. New Zealand, South Africa's rivals in the final, had a stronger team on paper, but South Africa did play with a one-man advantage, as Small had said, and the game was a thriller.

No one who saw it will ever forget seeing Mandela emerge onto the field wearing the green Springbok jersey with the number 6 on it, Francois Pienaar's number, and the green Springbok cap. The baffled silence in the stadium matched the stupefaction among the hundreds of millions watching the game on television in South Africa and around the world. I remember being stunned by the boldness of it and, for a tantalizing moment, by the recklessness of it, too. What if the gesture backfired? He had taken a massive risk. At least 90 percent of the people in the stadium were white. The rugby types were not known to be the most progressive sector of the South African population, but, rather, the blunt epitome of retrograde racism. Would they bluntly tell Mandela to "gaan kak," an Afrikaans expression that Mandela himself actually taught me, and which he politely translated as "Go to hell"?

Nobody watching inside the stadium could quite believe what they were seeing. I imagine they were all doing as I was, processing the meaning of this staggering apparition, rubbing their eyes, pondering what the response should be. Here was Mandela, the once-imprisoned martyr and living symbol of black resistance, in Springbok green. What to do? Heap derision on him? Abuse? Or perhaps simply ignore him and save up energy for the serious business ahead when the players, who were still in the locker room then, burst onto the field.

Mandela himself had no doubts. Somehow he knew—he had the measure of the Afrikaners, he had plumbed the depths of their souls. "I was convinced," he told me, "convinced that me wearing that jersey would have a terrific impact." Though he did confess that, even so, the reality of what happened exceeded all his expectations. What Mandela did with that gesture was to elicit a commensurate response from his ancient tormentors. Or, rather, they not only reciprocated, they gave back more, by joining in the most remarkable, most spectacularly unexpected chant I have ever heard. It began with a low, hesitant murmur then rose to a giant roar. No South African old enough to have been around then will ever forget it. The manager of the Springbok team, Morné du Plessis, a former Springbok captain who had endured the boos of black South African crowds and the boos of foreign crowds, captured the moment better than anyone.

"I walked down the players' tunnel in this bright, harsh winter sunlight," recalled du Plessis, his eyes red with tears,

needless to say, "and at first I could not make out what was going on, what the people were chanting, why there was so much
excitement before the players had even gone out onto the field.
Then I made out the words. This crowd of white people, of
Afrikaners, as one man, as one nation, they were chanting,
'Nel-son! Nel-son! Nel-son!' Over and over, 'Nel-son! Nel-son!
And well, it was just . . ." Tears ran down the big rugby man's
cheeks as he struggled to find the right words. "I don't think,"
du Plessis continued, "I don't think I'll ever experience a moment like that again. It was a moment of magic; it was a moment of wonder. It was the moment I realized that there really
was a chance this country could work. This man was showing
that he could forgive, totally, and now they—white South Africa, rugby white South Africa—they showed in that response
to him that they too wanted to give back, and that was how
they did it, chanting, 'Nelson! Nelson!'

"Then I looked at Mandela there in the green jersey, waving the Springbok cap in the air, waving and waving it, wearing that big, wide, special smile of his. He was so happy. He
was the image of happiness. He laughed and he laughed and
I thought, if only we have made him happy for this moment;
that is enough."

Mandela continued to laugh all those years later when I
interviewed him. Du Plessis and most of the other white South
Africans I spoke with continued to cry. Francois Pienaar
cried. James Small cried. Hennie le Roux and Balie Swart, also
Springbok players, cried. Kobie Coetsee and John Reinders
cried when I asked them about the 1995 rugby final. Koos Botha cried.

So did a man I never met, but whose story, told to me by
a friend who was in the stadium that day, has always stayed
with me. South Africa won the final, and when Mandela
walked out onto the field once again to hand the World Cup

to the Springbok captain, the roar arose again, this time with even more feeling: "Nel-son! Nel-son! Nel-son! Nel-son!" My friend in the stadium was sitting alongside a group of caricature Afrikaners, pot-bellied types in khaki shorts and shirts, replicas of the bitter-enders whom I had seen two years earlier summoning General Viljoen to lead them in their white freedom struggle. Now, they were shouting Mandela's name with all their might, save for one, who was too moved to join in the chanting. Tears streaming down his eyes, he mumbled to himself in Afrikaans, over and over, "That's my president . . . That's my president . . ."

What were these tears all about? I think they revealed a soft, susceptible core always lurking under the gruff Afrikaner exterior; I think it was guilt washing away, that guilt Zelda La Grange said all Afrikaners shared. Mandela did not just redeem black South Africa from tyranny; he redeemed white South Africa of its sins. The rugby World Cup final was a sporting contest, a political event, and a religious ceremony all thrown into one, with Mandela as the high priest dispensing absolution on behalf of his people. The tears shed not just in the stadium but in sitting rooms and bars all over South Africa were tears of repentance, gratitude, and relief. The act of atonement, the implicit bargain Mandela offered and they accepted, was to acknowledge him as their rightful leader and, in paying him homage, recognize all black South Africans as equal compatriots. Mandela extended the hand of fellowship to white South Africans and they took it. In so doing, as Koos Botha, the repentant terrorist put it, they set themselves free. "Free from guilt," he said, "free from fear, freedom from my past, free to live my life from here on with a good conscience."

The high sacramental point of the ceremony came when Mandela handed the big gold World Cup to Pienaar and the two of them celebrated together, raising their arms in the air with a euphoria that every South African of every hue shared. "Pienaar was our captain but, Mandela, well, he was more than just our president," Koos Botha said. "He was the leader of our people. He was the king of South Africa . . . And to think that we had been wanting our separate 'state of Israel!' And then it turns out that it's Mandela who gives us our state of Israel!"

Mandela and Pienaar had a brief exchange of words as one handed the other the cup. It was a pity nobody heard it at the time. I learned later that Mandela said to Pienaar, "Thank you for what you have done for our country," and Pienaar, with immense presence of mind, shot back, "No, Mr. President, thank you for what you have done for our country." Mandela had never looked so euphoric, not even on the day he walked out of prison. It was the happiest day of his political life and, personally, quite possibly the most thrilling.

"I was so tense," he said, chortling in recollection of the events at Ellis Park on June 24, 1995. "I kept on looking at my watch to see, 'Now when is this thing coming to an end?' I felt like fainting." And then when the game ended, how did he react? "Well," he said, and then he started to laugh so hard he could not get his sentence out. Collecting himself, he continued, "Do you know Louis Luyt?"

I did know Louis Luyt. He was the president of the South African rugby federation, a famously grumpy Afrikaner, who had only belatedly and grudgingly made some sort of peace with Mandela's new South Africa.

"Well," Mandela continued, struggling still to get the words out, "when the final whistle blew and we had won, Luyt and I . . . we just . . . suddenly . . . found ourselves embracing!" He made the gesture of folding someone in his arms and sputtered, "Me . . . me, and Louis Luyt . . . embracing!!"

No black South African I talked to about the rugby World Cup final shed any tears, but, like Mandela, all smiled and most laughed. The elections the year before had been the victory they had always sought; the ceremony at the rugby game put the seal on it. I feared that Archbishop Tutu, who finds reason for laughter in almost everything, might fall off his chair on each of the two occasions I talked to him about that day.

"Man," he said, "that victory did for our country more than all the sermons an archbishop could ever preach. I mean, who would ever have imagined that people would be dancing in the streets in Soweto? For a rugby victory? Of a Springbok side? 'Oh, get off it, man!' But they did! And, you know, can you imagine, here is a black guy, a black president who, just a few years ago, was the number-one terrorist for most white people!" Tutu was almost raving with excitement and disbelief. "I mean," he continued, "if you had . . . if you had predicted what actually happened there people would have said, ah, 'Do you . . . do you have a psychiatrist, please?' Because that was something totally unimaginable, that that crowd of White South Africans should . . . I mean, taking the roof off calling out 'Nelson! Nelson! Nelson!' for a black man, shouting out like that for a black president, who had been on Robben Island for twenty-seven years. It can't be true. But it *was*!"

If you had told me when I arrived in South Africa six years before the final, that the most recalcitrant sector of the white population would stand up in a rugby stadium and chorus Mandela's name, I, along with every other South African, would have said you were stark, raving mad.

Koos Botha captured the historical perspective of it all. "You know," he said, "in growing up we didn't actually mingle with black people, we didn't touch one another, we didn't hug one another, but that day . . . that's what I mean by saying it set us free. We were hugging one another and saying 'What a show this was!' "

Mandela did not take part in the show that night, preferring to follow the jubilant scenes at home on television. "You know," he said, "I did not expect it. I did not expect it! They were marching everywhere, in Soweto, in Katlehong, in the Transkei, in Houghton." His self-effacing reflex forbade him from claiming any more credit for the events of that day, but the laugher gave him away. "I was delighted. Very delighted. Yes, it was a day to remember." And, yes, if he were to reveal his personal feelings, it was now, in recollection of a moment whose memory he would savor to the end of his days. He never scored a more spectacular success. For no greater success was possible in Mandela's eyes than to do as he had done: inspire a whole nation to show the human animal at its best.

# 8

# MAGNANIMITY

I was with Mandela for the last time in December 2009, when I spent an hour with him at his home in Johannesburg. He was ninety-one years old. It was a bittersweet visit, because I knew I'd never see him again face to face, but also because he was living in a haze and it was clear he had been for some time. His short-term memory was fading and his mind wandered in and out.

Two uniformed policemen let me in at the gate. He had moved to another house in the same neighborhood since the last time I had seen him. It was smaller and less bright. I entered a large dining room where he sat at the head of a long table with his back to me. His hair was white and thinning. It was around one in the afternoon and outside the sun shone brightly, but the big room was dimly lit and he was all alone, still as a statue. He could barely walk, I had been told, and there were days when he did not get out of bed. It was quiet as a church in there and, as I approached him, I felt disconcerted at the thought that this time the sphinx would not spring to life, that he would be lost in the fog of old age.

Unable to stand, he turned his shoulders stiffly in my direction and shone upon me a flicker of his old thousand-volt smile. He reached out his hand—as enormous and tough-skinned as I remembered it from our first handshake nineteen years earlier—and he said: "Hello, John. How are you?" Zelda la Grange, his ever-loyal personal assistant, had introduced us, mentioning my name, so, while I wanted to believe he recognized me, I cannot say for sure that he did.

Before him was a plate of untouched minced meat. Forgetting me, he turned his gaze down upon his fork, as if debating whether to rise to the challenge of lifting it to his mouth. He was wearing one of his famous, shiny shirts, in brown and gold. His face had shrunk and become birdlike since I had last seen him; his frame was thin and brittle-boned, but he did not slump over the table, as someone his age might have been expected to do. His neck remained strong, his head erect as ever, his bearing unbowed. While he did not seem troubled or unhappy to receive a visitor, he was confused. For two or three minutes after the initial introduction, maybe more, no words passed his lips. It was awkward and, not for the first time, I wondered whether an eagerly anticipated encounter with Mandela would prove to be a disappointment.

Zelda helped spark a flicker in him. "Come on, khulu, eat up!" she said. "Come, khulu, you need to eat." Recalling that he had sometimes liked to joke about how women were always bossing him about, I made a crack along those lines, speaking loudly, close to his ear, for his hearing was not what it used to be. He let out a little smile, chuckled faintly and said, "Yes, that is true. Very true."

A connection had been made, but the triumph was short lived. He drifted off again, not to return for a while, a chance for me to reflect, as I do now, on why the man before whom I was so privileged to be sitting had been the greatest political figure of his age. I kept some notes from that last encounter, furiously scribbled immediately afterward, on the way back to my hotel. Among other things, I jotted down some words, vaguely remembered, lines from a speech he gave at the annual conference of the British Labour Party in 2000. Addressing a vast hall, he had said: "I can see men and women who are worthy candidates to immortality. When their last day comes we will be able to say here lies a man or a woman who has done his or her duty to country and to people. We will inter them into the earth but their names will live for eternity." Everybody present knew that the words were best interpreted as a premonitory epitaph for Mandela himself.

As he sat quizzically over his uneaten lunch, not much remained beyond a glimmer of the man who had bent an entire country to his will, who had persuaded black and white South Africans to abandon their vengeful impulses and their fears, who had got them to change their minds. He was a great seducer or, as others have described him, a brilliant salesman. Above all, he was a leader who led. He did not take his cue from opinion polls, nor did he pander to shifting public moods. He had fixed values: justice, equality, respect for all. He had a defined objective: to overthrow apartheid and establish in his country a system of one person, one vote. And he had a clear vision, after coming out of prison, of how to get there: by reconciling old enemies and forging a lasting peace between them.

As I have tried to set out in this book, he won over everyone he met. He got me, he got the rest of the press, he got his own followers, he got the high officeholders of the government that had jailed him, he got those who wished he had been hung instead of jailed, and he wrapped it all up at the rugby World Cup final when he captured the hearts of every South African.

What were the ingredients he possessed that rendered

everybody—not excluding the queen of England or the president of the United States—helpless to resist him?

First, he came across as a man of rock-hard integrity to all those he met, an initial impression that he never betrayed. Consistency is the key. Integrity may best be measured in terms of the coherence between the values one espouses and one's outward behavior in all aspects of life. What you saw with Mandela was what you got. He said he was generous and generous he was, way beyond any political or otherwise self-serving necessity. Whether making time to attend an old comrade's birthday party at a time when the duties of the presidency consumed every hour of his day, or traveling across country to see his old jailer after his son had died.

Second, Mandela treated everyone with respect. Leavened with a suggestion of flattery, sprinkled with a dash of courtesy, it got Mandela a long way. He doled respect out to everybody in equal measure irrespective of their station in life. It didn't matter if he was dealing with royalty, with foreign heads of government, with generals who planned to go to war against him, with gardeners, with flight attendants, with the unemployed or even with journalists.

I remember that, in April 1994, when South Africa's first democratic elections were less than three weeks away, but we still did not know whether they would go ahead, Mandela held a crisis meeting at a game lodge deep in the Kruger Park. He and President de Klerk strove to persuade Buthelezi to stop fighting, get talking, and take part in the vote. The meeting dragged on and on, way behind schedule, until two in the morning, when a long-awaited press conference was finally held. There was not much for Mandela or the others to tell us, for the meeting had been a catastrophic failure. Yet, when the press conference began, the first thing he did was to apologize to the long-suffering journalists for the delay. He leaned over to a journalist he knew, Debora Patta, and said, "Debora. I am most concerned. Have you eaten?"

Mandela had charisma. He inspired awe and admiration. Tony O'Reilly, an Irish businessman and the man whose butler would attend Mandela's presidential inauguration, defined it better than I could. "He had the true nobility of naturalness and so it was not a conscious mental effort. The Americans will have written forty doctoral dissertations and more self-help books analyzing the attributes required to impose your personality and make friends and influence people. But Mandela is a natural chieftain. He has tremendous self-confidence. He is convinced always that people will like him. He has that absolute assumption and if you have that assumption, you give off those vibrations we call charisma. He had an antiviral in his system that made him believe the world liked him." Unfortunately for the writers of doctoral dissertations and self-help manuals, high-wattage charisma on a Mandela scale is something you are either born with or, perhaps in some cases, raised with as a child. It is natural, as O'Reilly indicated, or it is nothing at all.

Walter Sisulu spotted it the first time he met Mandela in 1946. Sisulu was a labor organizer six years older than Mandela, with more than a decade's experience in black politics. Mandela was a young man, freshly arrived in Johannesburg from rural Transkei, with barely a political thought in his head. Yet Sisulu was impressed, glimpsing in Mandela a rare radiance and self-possession. "He happened to strike me more than any person I had met," Sisulu told me. "His demeanor, his warmth . . . I was looking for people of caliber to fill positions of leadership and he was a godsend to me." Sisulu recruited him to the liberation cause then and there, but he confessed he had little notion then of how right he would be. As for Mandela, he would joke when he was in prison and for years afterwards that, had he never met Sisulu, he would have spared himself a lot of trouble in life.

Finally, Mandela possessed extraordinary empathy. As a tool of leadership, empathy is beneficial twice over, for it combines generosity with the ability to make political gains. Mandela internalized his enemies' fears and aspirations, made plain to them that he understood them and, being able to imagine himself in their skin, managed to win gratitude and esteem, while positioning himself to hold the upper hand in negotiations. The Afrikaner leaders he sat down with succumbed to his spell, but they never understood his thought processes as completely as he did theirs. He saw further into their minds than they did into his. Niel Barnard implicitly recognized as much when he spoke to me of Mandela's "almost animal instinct for tapping into people's vulnerabilities and reassuring them."

These four qualities—integrity, respect, charisma, and empathy—are why Mandela conquered the hearts and minds of everybody he met. Translating those attributes into political success rested, however, on the rationality of his thought processes. All the talk one hears from his admirers all over the world about his saintlike generosity and absence of bitterness can, however true, obscure a more important factor in understanding Mandela: he was, as Richard Stengel, who ghostwrote Mandela's autobiography, perfectly put it, "the most pragmatic of idealists." Had he judged that violence was the most effective way to end apartheid, he would have taken that route (as he once did). In prison, he had the time to ponder that there was a better way, while also acquiring the self-knowledge to understand that pursuing peaceful means was more in tune with his temperament and his talents.

Mandela had his feet on the ground, he knew his objective,

and he knew how to get there. He was too alert to the haphaz-
ard twists that shape human life to attach himself inflexibly to
the unforgiving dogmas of ideology. He did not allow utopian
dreams or the emotions of the moment to cloud his political
eyesight. He was shrewd and tough-minded—not a romantic
or, much less, a fanatic. He was cunning or, as a British ambas-
sasor who knew him well once told me, he was "far craftier"
than most people imagined. But he had core principles that he
would not compromise. He refused, for example, the offer he
received from President Botha for his conditional release from
prison in 1986, appealing as the prospect might have been to
him personally. To have accepted renouncing violent means
to overthrow apartheid would have meant betraying the principle that only free men can negotiate. Once out of prison, he
refused to submit to President de Klerk's proposal when negotiations began to construct a *sui generis* democracy in which
white votes would count more than black votes. To achieve his
goals, he made pacts with plenty of devils. With Botha, with
Barnard, Coetsee, de Klerk, Viljoen, Buthelezi, even with the
chief of the apartheid defense force, General Georg Meiring,
whom he kept in place after becoming president.

The cordial relationship he had with one individual regarded far and wide as especially devilish caused much consternation among western governments. Ignoring appeals
from the United States and Britain, among others, he refused
to abandon his friendship with the Libyan dictator Muammar
Gaddafi. For Mandela, it was a matter of principle combined
with practicality. When Mandela was released and the rest of
the ANC leadership returned from exile, they badly needed
money to pay the rent on new headquarters, utility bills, and
staff salaries. Gaddafi came through. As far as Mandela was
concerned, the ANC was fighting a tyranny: the source of the

money he used to combat apartheid was not nearly as important as the fight itself.

It was hypocrisy to attack him for not renouncing Gaddafi, Mandela believed, the Western powers having done deals with him themselves in recent memory. Besides, there was a principle of loyalty involved. Mandela had stuck by his old jailer friends long past his hour of need; he would stick by Gaddafi, too. If anyone didn't like it, as he famously declared once at a press conference alongside President Bill Clinton, "They could jump in the pool." Clinton, to his credit, bent over with laughter.

Far more of a problem for Mandela than Gaddafi was his second wife, Winnie. And not just in the personal sphere. A significant test of Mandela's ability to impose pragmatic restraint on his emotions came when he had to address the political role she would play as the elections drew near, a time when relations between the two still remained sour. By the electoral system of proportional representation (agreed upon in the new constitution), each political party had to conduct an internal poll of its members prior to the 1994 elections to determine which of them would be elected to parliament. It was, in effect, an ANC popularity contest. Mandela won the most votes and so was ranked number one; Winnie was ranked sixth. I asked Mandela at a press conference held in January 1994, just after the results of the vote became public, how it was that an organization committed to human rights, as the ANC was, could have a convicted child kidnapper so high up on its electoral list. There were another half dozen ANC leaders sitting alongside Mandela. I remember one covered his face with his hands and others looked at me as if I were out of my mind. Winnie was a taboo subject, even among themselves.

Acknowledging the point, Mandela nodded sharply and replied: "Some may not like it, but there is a principle here of democratic accountability which is more important than what may or may not be the wishes of certain ANC leaders." It was a convincing reply that allowed those certain leaders sitting by his side to breathe again. At the end of the press conference, Mandela sought me out. He was as aware as I was of the little moment of tension I had generated, but he made no mention of it, limiting himself to shaking my hand, giving me his big smile, and asking me if had had an enjoyable Christmas with my family. His bridge-building instinct had kicked in. I have no reason to doubt his curiosity as to the kind of Christmas I had enjoyed, but he was also keeping a journalist on his side. Pragmatism, one more time.

Politics is not a terrain of spotless moral hygiene, and politics was the terrain Mandela inhabited. The success of his mission was based on cutting deals and making compromises. One side cedes and the other side cedes, so that both can come out winning. It is a lesson that the Israelis and the Palestinians have patently failed to absorb in their countless attempts at negotiations since the much-trumpeted Oslo Accords. Mandela applied the principle not only in his negotiations with the enemy, but also when the time came to exercise the law. By any standard notion of justice, the perpetrators of what the United Nations labeled a crime against humanity should all have ended up in jail. If Mandela was imprisoned for twenty-seven years, Botha, Barnard, and even de Klerk, as well as the totality of the military and police high command who enforced apartheid, should have been locked up for longer. But Mandela knew that to do that would have risked a backlash that would have put the stability of the new democracy in danger.

So instead, on becoming president, he appointed a Truth and Reconciliation Commission, which offered amnesty to apartheid-era wrongdoers in exchange for the confession of crimes. Catharsis, in other words, in place of retribution.

Mandela understood that, as Voltaire said, the best can be the enemy of the good, that if you stick stubbornly to your optimum position, determined to settle only for your ideal of perfection, the chances are that you'll fail in your objective, while running the risk that peace will turn to war. Underlying everything was a sober assessment of how far he could go in his objectives given the balance of power between himself and his rivals. As he said once after becoming president, "Reconciliation is a strategy based on realism, for none of the former enemies has vanquished the other."

Mandela's notion of realism extended to a refusal to accept the lion's share of the credit for the success of the South African transition. He would often insist that the decision to opt for the pragmatic route, sacrificing notions of perfect justice, was a collective one. He was adamant that the rest of the leadership of the ANC should receive their due, arguing as much on one particularly forceful occasion in an article he wrote for the *Johannesburg Sunday Times* in February 1996. It came in response to an editorial the previous week in which the same newspaper attributed the South African miracle to Mandela, not least to his warmth and generosity.

"If only to emphasize that I am human, and as fallible as anyone else, let me admit that these accolades do flatter me," Mandela wrote. "The compliment is genuinely appreciated, as long as it does not present the President as 'superhuman' and create the impression that the ANC—with its thousands of leaders and millions of supporters—is a mere rubber stamp of my ideas; and that the ministers, experts, and others are all insignificant, under the magic spell of a single individual."

Of course, Mandela was not operating in a vacuum. His millions of supporters were the source of his strength and he would not have gotten where he did without the arguments and opinions of the gifted tacticians alongside him in the ANC leadership. It was ANC policy to negotiate, to seek reconciliation and to forgive, and the bedrock principle of the ANC had always been what they called "non-racism." Yet the ANC's national executive, members of whom I have known well, would never have managed to sell their policies as successfully as they did without the leader whom they all acknowledged as the first among equals.

There was free democratic debate within the ANC's national executive, but up to a point. Mandela's style of leadership could be imperious. The gambit employed by the shrewder souls at these meetings was to aim their arguments specifically at Mandela, and insinuate their way into his thought processes through the careful study of his moods and via an understanding of the issues on which he was never prepared to bow. Whatever decision was reached in their debates, it would bear Mandela's personal stamp.

As for the ANC's "non-racism," the principle on which every strategy was built, the first time I interviewed Mandela, before he became president, he had said to me that the African people were by nature very kind and well-disposed toward white people and that ANC policy was an expression of such sentiments. It was certainly my experience as a white man who continually went into black townships, often at times of extreme violence, that people in almost all cases treated me in accordance with the merits of my behavior, not as a function of the color of my skin. But it was also true that before Mandela went to jail, a rival black organization called the Pan-Africanist Congress threatened to capture the support of the majority of black people. The PAC's slogan, the very opposite of non-racism, was "one settler, one bullet." If the PAC had had a leader with Mandela's powers in 1990, the history of South Africa might have turned out very differently. If, in the end, the gentler nature of black South Africans prevailed over vengeful impulses, it was in large part because Mandela did with black South Africans as he did with white: he drew out the best they had inside them. It was Mandela who tilted the balance in favor of peace.

The truth is that, for all Mandela's protestations, he really was South Africa's indispensable man. As Archbishop Tutu said, "We couldn't have done it without him."

Have they been able to do it without him since he retired from active politics? There is much to lament about the ANC, which remains in power two decades after Mandela became president. His successors, Thabo Mbeki and Jacob Zuma, were always going to struggle to fill his shoes, yet there is a general sense that they could have governed so much better than they have. South Africa creeps up every year in the global corruption rankings, the crime statistics are shocking, and the government has failed dismally to address problems in education and policing. Such disappointments are, always and everywhere, the regrettable nature of things. It is infantile as well as unhistorical to imagine that the exemplary episode South Africa lived under Mandela would presage inexorable progress towards some illusory utopia. To argue that his image is retrospectively tarnished by the cynicism or incompetence of those who came after him is equally wrongheaded.

Mandela did the job that his time demanded and, quite apart from the moral and political example he bequeathed, he left a legacy for which every South African should give thanks. He stopped a civil war from happening and built a democracy that remains as stable as it is fundamentally sound, however many issues of day-to-day governance remain unresolved. Things may change, for the better or for the worse. But, as of today, South Africa is a country where freedom of speech is respected, where the judiciary remains independent, where elections have been incontestably free and fair.

Thanks also in good measure to Mandela, South Africa is not today a country where race is the defining issue of political life, as it was when I arrived there in 1989. I still travel continually to South Africa and I believe that, taking into account the stubbornly residual tribalism of the population, it is a place now where everyday relations between black and white people are as uncomplicated as anywhere else I know—even including the United States, where I lived for nearly four years after leaving South Africa. Much of the credit belongs to black South Africans, who Mandela correctly identified to me as a people extraordinarily lacking in racial resentment, but much also belongs to him. After he became president, he became a leader to all South Africans. In 2007, when a bronze statue of Mandela was unveiled in London's Parliament Square alongside statues of Abraham Lincoln and Winston Churchill, I remember reading a caption under a photograph of Mandela in a British newspaper describing him as a black leader. I was taken aback. The adjective felt as gratuitously out of place as if "white leader" had been used to describe Lincoln or Churchill. I realized that I had long since stopped regarding Mandela as belonging to any racial group.

Am I too effusive in my admiration of Mandela? Too defensive, for that matter, of his legacy? I do sometimes ask myself these questions. There are a number of perfectly intelligent people who refuse to succumb to what they regard as the "Mandela myth." I have a simple response to Mandela's few detractors, the same response I give myself when I entertain some brief moments of doubt. Who am I, or anybody else, to question Mandela's greatness when the likes of Constand Viljoen and Niel Barnard, in their day among the most right-wing extremists on the planet, fall at his feet? He is their hero, as he is the hero of practically all South Africans, as he is a hero, and shall remain one, to the world. Not least in this day and age when heroes, at least in the political arena, are in short supply.

In an excellent book, *Heroes*, Lucy Hughes-Hallet examines a number of legendary figures, among them Achilles, Garibaldi, Ulysses, and El Cid. She does not include Mandela in her book, but his image, she writes, "conforms more closely than that of almost any other public figure of the recent past to the ancient ideal of the hero." What all true heroes have in common, she continues, is that they are "seductive and dynamic," they are "glamorous and brilliant," they have "courage and integrity and a disdain for the cramping compromises by means of which the un-heroic majority manage their lives." Mandela, the prisoner turned redeemer, fits the bill perfectly.

I recently came across a definition of leadership by the late American novelist David Foster Wallace that could have been written with Mandela in mind. "Effective leaders," wrote Wallace, "are individuals who help us overcome the limitations of our own selfishness and weaknesses and fears and get us to do harder, better, more important things than we can get ourselves to do on our own."

Where Mandela failed was in getting the best out of his own family. He perceived his role preeminently as an instrument of others, as a servant of the South African people. As the years that followed show, it was no idle rhetoric. At high personal cost, he made every other aspect of his life subservient to his political mission. And I believe he ended his days considering that, on balance, the price had been worth paying. That, at any rate, was the conclusion with which I left that final meeting with him at his home. For a moment did come when he sprang, almost mystically, to life.

I had been trying for some time to spark the old engine of

his mind into action, but he just sat there, serene and vacant. Until I mentioned the name of one man who I had come to admire far more than I would ever have imagined the first time I saw him. He was a man who, by an accident of fortune, had been born into a particular country, at a particular time with a particular color of skin, but whom Mandela regarded, within those narrow limits, to be a man of true integrity. For, and this is another of the secrets of his success, Mandela understood that people were not born evil, that racial or national stereotypes were dangerous lies.

I mentioned General Constand Viljoen. "Ah, yes," Mandela said, his eyes suddenly lighting up. "The military man . . ." Excited, encouraged to pursue this track, I mentioned the name of Niel Barnard. "Yes, yes!" he whispered. Then I mentioned Kobie Coetsee. "Ah, yes . . . very good." I had felt until now as if I had traveled to a cavern to visit an ancient monk in search of wisdom, but the monk was in a trance from which it seemed impossible to wake him. Then, suddenly, awake Mandela did.

The mention of his old Afrikaner enemies set his wheels in motion. I could see him thinking, delving into his past. In a thin but steady voice the sentences began to form. "My people said I was afraid," he began. "They said I was a coward because I reached out to the Afrikaner." He paused, trying to recall what his response had been. Then he continued. "But I did not engage them in the debate. I said nothing to them. I knew I was right. I knew this was the way to peace. And after some time they understood I was right. They have seen the results. We have peace."

There it was. The boldness and the vision he had shown in engaging in dialogue with the apartheid state's Afrikaners, for which he was roundly criticized internally. And there, too, was his stubborn conviction that the only way to achieve his lifetime goal and avert a bloodbath had been to engage with his old enemies. And, yes, in the end they all did understand that he was right. He killed apartheid with kindness, and he gave birth to a country that found peace.

Mandela stopped talking as abruptly as he had begun, but, suddenly, he started picking, at last, at his food. That sudden burst of light was, however, as much as I was going to get out of him. For what remained of our encounter, he concentrated his remaining faculties on the challenge of feeding his frail body. I prattled away gamely enough, getting scant response, and then we said good-bye. He looked up, took my hand and gave me the parting gift of that smile of his, and then I left.

As sad as I was to say good-bye, it was also a moment to give thanks for the extraordinary good fortune and privilege I had had in getting to know him a little and to have been exposed for a portion of my life to his light.

What had I learned from him? Many things, but two stand out. First, he taught me the greatest of human values. I named my only son James Nelson after my father and after Mandela, and since he learned to speak I have tried to teach him that the most important thing in life is to be kind. I do not expect him to change the world, but I would like him to be the sort of person who would show the same generous decency to people as Mandela showed to Christo Brand or John Reinders.

The second lesson Mandela taught me is as simple as it is rare to find: that one can be a very great politician and a very great person at the same time. Admired and liked, he was the antithesis of malignancy in power, the polar opposite of a leader who deployed his talent for moving multitudes to bring out the worst in human nature.

I once asked Archbishop Tutu, whose judgment on Mandela I value more than that anyone else I know, if he could sum up Mandela for me in a few words. He did it in one. "Magnanimity," he replied. Tutu was right. Mandela was big-hearted and generous in the use of the power he commanded, and as a man, too. I could only hope as I left his home that last time, as he faced the end of his life, that he remained just lucid enough to understand that one last triumph still awaited him, one final measure of his achievement: that his death would be mourned and his life would be celebrated equally among his compatriots, black and white.

I carry with me a tapestry of memories of Mandela. But one image stays with me above all others. He was at the very peak of his faculties, a young seventy-five, and he sat before me, just after becoming president in the same office as the white presidents who had jailed him and humiliated his people. It felt as if, at that very moment, he had finally digested the enormity of what he had done. He had just observed that a matter of weeks earlier black and white people had been standing together in line, chatting to each other, as they waited to cast their votes at his country's first democratic elections. Pausing to reflect on that image with gratitude and satisfaction, and with affection for his fellow men, he smiled and said, "It is really remarkable. . . ." He smiled again and looked away, as if imagining himself back in his lonely cell, or recalling the time of his release, when he still had what seemed like an impossible mountain to climb. He was sitting beside me, but alone in his thoughts, savoring the consummation of a lifelong dream. His voice trailed off, but the smile remained. "Remarkable," he repeated. "Remarkable, remarkable. . . . Yes, remarkable."

# ACKNOWLEDGMENTS

In the first instance I must thank my old friend James Lemoyne, who knows me so well he knew I had to write this book before I did. It was his idea that I should do it, and he was a source of constant encouragement and valuable insights as I set about the task.

My agent Anne Edelstein was even sharper on the draw than usual in getting this book out to the publishing world and also proved to be my trusty first line of editorial defense. Not for the first time, she has acted above and beyond the call of duty.

My editor at HarperCollins, David Hirshey, his assistant, Sydney Pierce, and other members of his team, not least Susan Amster, the eagle-eyed lawyer, performed skilled, Trojan labor on this manuscript, improving my words and honing my thoughts with rare persistence and rigor. It was an immense comfort and a pleasure to be in such good hands.

I should also note my debt to the various colleagues I worked alongside in the making of a number of film documentaries about Mandela, notably Cliff Bestall, Indra Delanerolle, and David Fanning. A fair chunk of the material in this book was gleaned during the work we did together.

Finally, a special thanks to my friend Michael Shipster, who really knows his stuff on Mandela and South Africa, and was kind enough to read the original manuscript and offer plenty of choice improvements on it. Thanks as well, and as ever, to Sue Edelstein and to my son James Nelson Carlin, who I hope will read this book one day (or else!) and learn the supreme value of kindness from his immortal namesake.